ALWAYS A PLEASURE

Chuck Swirsky

Copyright © 2022 Chuck Swirsky

Published in the United States by
Eckhartz Press
Chicago, Illinois

All rights reserved.

No part of this book may be used or reproduced in any manner whatsoever without written permission except in the case of brief quotations embodied in critical articles and reviews.

ISBN: 979-8-9861972-4-1

"When I first met Chuck I didn't believe anyone could be that positive and supportive. Add that to enthusiastic and genuine and you have Chuck Swirsky. A great basketball broadcaster and a better man."

– **Steve Stone**
1980 American League Cy Young Award Winner, Baltimore Orioles, Chicago White Sox TV baseball analyst

"I have now worked with Chuck "The Swirsk" for 14 years. First and foremost, he is a good man, great partner and loyal friend. I have not met a person who is more knowledgeable of the game of basketball, past and present. His recall is nothing short of amazing! He always has an impressive fact or stat that is relevant to our broadcast. He brings his 'A GAME' every time."

– **Bill Wennington**
Chicago Bulls, 3 time NBA Champion, basketball analyst on Chicago Bulls Radio Network

INTRODUCTION

For the last ten years I've been approached by agents, publishers, and fans imploring me to author a book detailing my career in sports broadcasting.

I put the thought of writing a book "on the shelf" until now. What caused me to change my mind? The 2022-2023 NBA season will mark my 25th season as an NBA broadcaster and my 50th year of combined high school, college, and professional sports broadcasting and play-by-play. It's time.

If someone told me I would be in my 25th season, fulfilling a lifelong goal of calling NBA games—something I wanted to do as a child, I would tell you that dreams do come true and to always follow your dreams. I'm a big believer in passion, perseverance, and hard work. Stay true to your heart. It's always about the heart. Everything is about the heart. I have been truly blessed.

This book encompasses not only my career but also people I have met along the way, sharing my views about the ever-changing landscape of sports and sports media. I hope you enjoy the book as much as I enjoy sharing my journey with you.

CHAPTER 1
THE EARLY YEARS

I was a baby-boomer generation child of the 1950s. The third of three children born to Paula and Arthur Swirsky in Norfolk, Virginia. Sisters Jane and Mary Lou preceded me, and we had a ton of fun growing up in a house full of love and good times.

My father's parents were born in Russia, my mother's parents in Sicily. My grandfather on my dad's side passed away prior to my birth, and I met my dad's mom only twice before her death. My mom's side of the family was Italian to the core. When we visited them in Ohio, it resulted in plenty of food and conversation. My mom was the oldest of five children and the only girl of the family. My mom was extremely bright, articulate, kind, and compassionate, deeply rooted in her Catholic faith. My mom was a career schoolteacher and loved every second of it. Without question, the two biggest influences in my life have not been men but women. My mom loved me unconditionally no matter how mischievous and immature I was.

Back in the 1960s, no one had ever heard of ADD or ADHD. Even though I received a negative test result as an adult, there is no question I have a trace of it in my DNA. I was an above average student but found myself more often than not talking out of turn, and probably for good reason I won the "Class Clown of the Year Award" multiple times. The penalty: The nuns made me go to the back of the classroom, facing the wall wearing a dunce cap. Seriously. A dunce cap. No chance that happens today.

On other occasions, it was being called to the front of the classroom and being spanked on the bottom or slapped across the knuckles with a ruler. Think that would fly today? That was the main course, followed by writing, "I will not talk out of turn" five hundred times. Those nuns at St. Pius in Norfolk, Virginia were as tough as the 1985 Bears defense, trust me!

The other person of significant character building was my grandmother Ipsaro. A self-taught woman who was strong, wise, opinionated, a fabulous cook, and a passionate woman of faith. She put me in my place more than once, and looking back on my life, I needed it. My grandmother and my mother, who left this world decades ago, shaped my life in every way possible, and it goes without saying I think about them every day.

As a military man, my father didn't make a lot of money, nor were he or my mom raised in a family of wealth. I really didn't complain because we had everything you could possibly want. We had a house in a cozy neighborhood and food on the table, enough said. My parents were hard-working people and we never, ever complained about our lifestyle. We loved to play kickball in front of the house or ride our bicycles to the park. They stressed education, reading in particular, but they also had a creative flair. Sunday was church day. My father was raised Lutheran but converted to Catholicism. More on my father later in the book.

Sunday church service was nonnegotiable. Attending Mass was something I actually enjoyed, and Catholic schools gave me a solid base in my formative years. After Mass, my mom prepared a full course brunch with a tablecloth setting. We all had specific chores ranging from setting the table to washing dishes. While my mom was making Sunday brunch, my two sisters and I would create our own play and present it to our parents after the meal. It was a mini five- to ten-minute performance, orchestrated especially for our parents on a weekly basis. My parents would also take us to historical sites in Virginia, and I cherish those moments as I reflect on my upbringing.

I thoroughly enjoyed my early years in Virginia, a state full of rich tradition and gorgeous beaches on the Atlantic Ocean.

CHAPTER 2
WELCOME TO THE WORLD OF SPORTS

My first remembrance of anything to do with sports of any kind was at four or five years old. I vividly recall going to a baseball game with friends of the family and seeing lush green grass and spotless white uniforms with red caps and red jersey numbers and trim. It was not a professional game. I'm thinking it was either Little League ball or a level or two above. It didn't matter. I watched in amazement, players running around a dirt infield touching what I thought at the time were "white pillows" that were actually bases. I saw players throw and catch a ball with a brown glove. I saw people clapping hands, shouting encouragement to players, and eating popcorn. I took it all in. One simple game opened a new world for me, one that I would never let go.

After that experience I wanted to return to the park and watch more games. I talked about sports all the time. Even at the age of five I knew that talking sports or playing sports was going to be my destiny. My identity, so to speak. My father was not a sports fan. He loved to tinker with our car, a 1955 Packard Clipper. He was a master handyman. He could fix anything. It didn't matter if it was a broken pipe under the sink, an issue with the house, or an electrical switch, my dad could get it done. He loved train sets, Lionel Trains to be specific.

His love of putting things together and taking them apart did not carry over to me. For Christmas, I would receive Erector set kits consisting of pieces of steel along with nuts and bolts to build things. My attempts were futile because my brain just couldn't function along those lines, nor did I have any interest. I could sense even at a young age my father was disappointed I didn't share his passion or similar interests.

My dad was a decorated U.S. Naval officer, and I loved going to the base with him and going aboard his ship, the USS Sierra. I loved everything about the Navy. He was a man of faith, character, and integrity. He was also a disciplinarian, and there was no grey area with his personality. You either got the job done correctly or you didn't. Every day after he returned from the Naval base, one of my chores was to polish his shoes. If there was one smudge or one place I missed, I had to do it again and get it right. Some may look at this as harsh, but honestly it was one of the best life lessons I ever received. Attention to details was everything to my dad. I attempt to apply that same mentality in every phase of my life. If you're going to do it, do it right. Don't go through the motions. Don't mail it in. No excuses.

My dad figured out quickly how much I loved sports and took me to my first professional baseball game, a Class A Carolina League contest featuring the Tidewater Tides and Peninsula Senators.

I loved playing sports in the neighborhood, whether it was in the street or in the park. After we moved from Virginia to Bellevue, Washington it was nonstop, playing wiffle ball, baseball, touch football, basketball, or street hockey. I loved the competition. I loved the concept of "team" and just enjoyed being outside with friends who had a common interest. I attempted to play organized football, but as a 10-year-old, reality set in when the equipment weighed more than I did. My mom signed me up for CYO (Catholic Youth Organization) basketball and Little League baseball, and I thrived in that environment.

Even though I was undersized, my favorite sport was basketball. I loved the game, loved the gym, loved the colors of uniforms. My mom would take me to her school's games at Norfolk Catholic High. When you're seven or eight years old you think high school players are the size of today's NBA players. I was in awe. With my dad away on assignment with Navy duties, I'd tag along with her to weekend school events, which always included some sort of athletic games.

I practiced ball handling and shooting skills almost every day of the year. The Seattle area brought plenty of rain, so I would dribble the ball in the garage, determined to get better. My neighbors across the street, the Pizzalato family, had a backyard court, and through their kindness I shot hoops with Alan, who was a grade behind me in school. Alan and his family were so gracious as they always included me in attending Seattle University, University of Washington, and Seattle Sonics games.

In the tenth grade a sign was posted on the gym wall for junior varsity basketball tryouts at Interlake High School. I wanted to make the team. I ate, slept, and dreamed of wearing the navy blue, Columbia blue, and white uniform of my high school. I wanted to feel the accomplishment of hard work and the acceptance of joining the "club" as a member of the team. It was not meant to be. I was cut the first day. The JV coach simply said I wasn't good enough.

Decades later, in my heart, I know I should have made the

team. For whatever reason, the coach decided otherwise. I am being totally honest here. I think about that decision every day. It still hurts. I have never let it go. That decision alone spurred me on to persevere and turn my attention to sports journalism.

My father never read the sports section, so I would take it when the paper arrived in late afternoon. I devoured stats, names, etc. I would go to bed with a flashlight tucked underneath the blanket, memorizing names and stats from The Sporting News. I'd listen to out-of-town ballgames blasting through a transistor radio, whether it was Bob Prince announcing Pirates games on KDKA in Pittsburgh or Harry Caray calling the play-by-play of the St. Louis Cardinals on KMOX in St. Louis. 20 years later I'd be working side-by-side with Harry at WGN Radio in Chicago. What a world! My percolating passion for sports was full speed ahead.

Some of my best life memories were those moments when we would just go out and play with no worries or stress. Life however isn't a straight line, as I soon learned the hard way at the age of twelve.

CHAPTER 3
ARE YOU GOING NORTH OR SOUTH

After retiring from the Navy, my father took a job at Lockheed Shipbuilding Company, using his engineering and leadership talents designing a sleek new vessel called a hydrofoil to assist Naval operations. With the Vietnam War escalating, the United States military was about to enter an unknown world of combat in Southeast Asia. My dad fought in two wars: World War 2 and the Korean War. He loved the United States of America. He loved putting on the Navy uniform. He loved serving his country, and he did it with pride every single day.

Politics was never discussed at home, but my mom was definitely pulling for a 1960 John F. Kennedy victory. My mom took me out of my first-grade class a week before the election, and I saw Kennedy address a huge crowd in Norfolk near her school. One of her students put me on his shoulders and I saw Kennedy deliver a speech some twenty yards from the stage. I remember watching the 1960 Democratic Convention on a black-and-white television along with the first-ever televised Presidential debates between Kennedy and Richard Nixon. During that period of time the NASA space program took flight literally and figuratively. The "Mercury Seven" were astronauts who would bring a new frontier to the world. It was captivating. President Kennedy promised to put a man on the moon by the end of the decade. Sadly, he never saw his dream come to fruition.

    Friday, November 22, 1963, left an indelible mark on my life. I was in the fourth grade at St. Pius X in Virginia when an announcement came over the loudspeaker from the student office informing classes that President Kennedy had been shot in Dallas, Texas. We were told to be silent as our teacher, Sister Francinus, led us in prayer. Some students were crying and weeping uncontrollably. Sister herself had tears but kept her composure. Minutes later, another announcement: President Kennedy was dead. Bedlam broke out with students running up and down the hallway. As teachers and staff got things under control, we were in total shock. Our nation was in mourning, as was our family. On Sunday after we returned from church, we turned on the TV, and moments later, Kennedy's alleged assassin Lee Harvey Oswald was gunned down on national TV. The TV was turned off as we were in disbelief over what had transpired in a 72-hour span in American history.

    My dad sensed that a way to bond with me was sports. It wasn't his thing, but he knew I loved to throw and catch any ball, loved going to games, and enjoyed fishing. On Friday, May 6, 1966, my dad asked me if I wanted to go to that night's Seattle Angels game (Seattle Angels were the Triple-A affiliate of the parent Angels ballclub). I was totally surprised. Very seldom would my dad go to a sporting event, but I jumped at the opportunity. We had a great time. I loved going to a baseball game, any sporting event, really. I loved spending one-on-one time with my dad.

    One week later he died of a heart attack.

It was Friday, May 13, 1966. It was just before noon. We had a school field trip earlier in the day and returned to Ivanhoe Elementary School in Bellevue, Washington. As we sat down for lunch, my sixth-grade schoolteacher Ed Filler was pulled aside by the school principal, holding a brief discussion outside the classroom. The principal departed and Mr. Filler asked me to join him outside. My first reaction was, "Ok, what did I do now?" My classmates were good-natured, giving it to me, laughing, thinking I was in trouble. I stepped outside the room and my teacher looked me in the eyes and said, "Charlie, I regret to inform you, your father died this morning." I blacked out. The next thing I remember I was in his car (he lived two blocks away) driving home. There were tons of vehicles at our house. I was crying as I entered the house full of neighbors, priests, and teachers from my mom's school with an inordinate amount of food that people so generously brought over.

I was numb. Even writing this chapter in the book, recapturing one of the darkest days I ever faced, brings sadness to my heart. I never got a chance to say goodbye to him. My dad was a great man. I'm forever thankful for his unconditional love, integrity, and character.

Two months later my mom and I had our first real talk following my dad's passing. As a family we were still grieving, which is natural and healthy. Even as a 12-year-old I realized that things were going to change on many levels. My mom sat me down, and somewhere in the talk about our new world my mom said, "Charlie, are you going north or are you going south?" I didn't know what that meant. She explained that this is a defining moment in our house, that I can apply my dad's work ethic and live a positive life, or I can feel sorry for myself and just deal with self-pity and excuses, something my father never put up with.

The conversation was a hard one. A difficult one. A needed one. But I struggled without my father in my life. He left this world way too soon, and one of my biggest regrets is that he never saw me achieve my goal as a professional broadcaster calling NBA games. As usual, my mom showed her wisdom, strength, and common sense. She was an incredible human being. I loved my parents so very much.

CHAPTER 4
THE MAGIC OF RADIO

A few miles from where we lived in Bellevue was an outdoor mall located in the center of town. It was full of clothing shops, retail venues, etc. It also featured a radio station, KFKF, which stood for the station owners, Katherine and Kemper Freeman. A United Press International terminal was encased outside the studio, and while my mom shopped, I stood squarely in front of it as it typed out sports news, scores, and news from around the country. I was addicted to the machine.

One day I found enough gumption to walk in unannounced, telling the receptionist, "I'd like to work here." I was 12 years old. The woman behind the desk smiled and jokingly had me fill out an application. Of course I didn't hear back, but I called the Sports Director, Bill O'Mara, and asked if I could meet with him to discuss radio broadcasting, which he agreed to do. To his credit, he gave me plenty of time and said if I cared to keep stats for him at various events, it would be a start.

Sure enough, my mom would drop me off at high schools in the area as I sat in the press box for the "KFKF King County

Game of the Week." Two years later, O'Mara surprised me by putting me on the air at halftime of a Sammamish-Bellevue high school football game. I know you'll find this hard to believe, but I was speechless for 15-20 seconds before I came to my senses announcing individual and team first half stats. That was my introduction to live radio at 14 years old. By the way, the "KingCo" Conference is comprised of high schools located east of Seattle and to this very day remains an extremely competitive league, one that produced Zach LaVine (Bothell High) and former NBA Coach Quinn Snyder (Mercer Island).

One of the first sportscasters that caught my ear and attention was Bill Schonely. Schonely was an outstanding play-by-play announcer who called a variety of sports including hockey. Schonely's description of the Seattle Totems of the Western Hockey League left a lasting impression on me. He also called University of Washington sports and teamed with Jimmy Dudley to call the Seattle Pilots in their one and only year of existence in Major League Baseball. Schonely later became the first voice of the Portland Trailblazers and is beloved by their loyal fan base even to this day at the age of 93. He called his last game in 1998. All told, he did a whopping 2,552 games. In 2012 he was inducted into the Basketball Hall of Fame.

During my junior year in high school I started looking at the next chapter of my life. I had the grades, but the question was money. My mom took on two additional jobs after my father passed away. In addition to her full-time position as a schoolteacher at St. Louise, she joined a theater company in Bellevue, performing on stage and working behind the scenes. She also worked in the gift shop at Overlake Hospital. As I said earlier, my mom was an incredible person who always put her children first. Even then college was expensive, and we just didn't have the type of money that would allow me to attend UCLA or University of Maryland (my first two choices). I became curious about Ohio University (NOT Ohio State, but Ohio University) and learned that the school featured an outstanding broadcast journalism program. My grandparents lived outside of Cleveland, some four hours north of Athens, Ohio. The school was willing to give me financial aid.

Ohio University, here I come!

In my humble opinion, Athens is one of the best-kept secrets on the planet. With its rolling hills, it's a fantastic place and an awesome campus.

My first day as a college student was a major wake-up call. My biggest high school class was no more than 25 students. My first class as a freshman in college was an 8 a.m. Introduction to the History of Radio/Television. Enrollment: 100. Was I intimidated? Absolutely.

Later that day, WOUB, the university's radio/television station invited students to an open house, specifically for those interested in sports broadcasting. The hallway was so jammed I could barely hear the student staff members speak. It was crazy, yet it was reality. Tons of competition ahead, and if this was something I really wanted to pursue, I better get used to it.

The staff consisted of Sports Director Bob Tayek, who went on to become the PA Voice of the now Cleveland Guardians. Joining him was Jack Briggs, who became the Sports Director and anchor for the Associated Press; Ken Broo, a Cincinnati sports radio/TV icon; and Bruce Johnson, who served as the long-time "Voice of Rutgers" athletics for two decades.

I learned how to write radio and TV scripts as well as understand the art of interviewing. You ASK questions and you listen. Simple, right? Wrong. Many reporters fall in a bad habit of making statements, expecting their interviewees to respond to them. Ask, listen, and follow up. Be engaged.

I got my first on-air shift during my winter quarter of my freshman year. The news anchor behind the glass introduced me as "Chuck" Swirsky. It was the first time someone had ever referred to me as "Chuck." It was always Charlie or "Swirsk." That's how "Chuck" started and stuck, but I prefer Charlie.

In October of my freshman year, I read that Oakland's Gene Tenace, fresh off his World Series MVP performance against the Cincinnati Reds, lived in Lucasville, Ohio about 75 miles from Athens. I called information, his phone number was listed, I introduced myself and said I'd like to bring a camera crew to his house for a brief interview. Remember, we're talking about the '72 A's, the start of a dynasty with three straight World Series titles. Tenace had a fabulous "Fall Classic," batting .348 with 4 homers and 9 RBI. We drove to his modest home, and there it was: in his garage, a brand-new car for being named MVP. One problem, the car had a bad engine and really wasn't drivable. But we did the interview, and it aired that night. He was terrific. I still can't believe at 18 years young I had the moxie to call the World Series MVP and conduct a one-on-one interview, but it gave me plenty of confidence.

While preparing sportscasts on WOUB radio we would call various local, regional, and national broadcasters hoping, check that, pleading in some cases, they would assist us by previewing or recapping a sporting event. A bright star was emerging in Cleveland by the name of Joe Tait, who came on the NBA scene with the expansion Cavaliers in 1970. Joe was familiar with WOUB and Ohio University as he served as Sports Director and oversaw the department in the late 1960s. Someone passed on Joe's phone number to me, and here's how it went down.

"Mr. Tait, this is Chuck Swirsky, WOUB Sports. I know it's probably an inconvenience, but could you give us a 30-45 second preview of tonight's Cavaliers game?"

Joe always came through. Not just some of the time. All of the time. Prior to my junior year, Joe helped me land an internship at WWWE Radio in Cleveland. I was working in the sports department writing afternoon drive-time copy for Steve Albert, producing and scheduling guests for iconic talk show host Pete Franklin, and hanging out in the booth during Cleveland MLB home games with Joe and Herb Score. All this because of a simple call looking for a 30-45 second voicer on a Cavaliers game. Albert, by the way, is the younger brother of Marv, and had a distinguished career calling NBA, NHL, WHA, MLB, and boxing events.

It was a self-made internship. I would be at the station at 9-10 a.m. and left at midnight. I am NOT exaggerating. I lived at my grandparents' house but hardly saw them because of my long but very rewarding hours. During the day I would book guests and then head to Joe's house, where I would pick his brain about the business. I was there almost every day when the baseball team was at home.

Joe became impactful in my life in so many ways as we kept in touch on a regular basis. You have no idea what I experienced when we met up for the first time as NBA broadcasters in 1999. All those years of mentoring and teaching had resulted in me becoming an NBA broadcaster. He was a great man and a great mentor. I met so many big-name wonderful play-by-play broadcasters during my two-year internship, from Dick Enberg of the Angels (who went on to network success calling Super Bowl XX) to Phil Rizzuto of the Yankees.

On Friday, August 2, 1974, the Indians played the Yankees. Fritz Peterson, the former Yankee, battled "Sudden" Sam McDowell, the former fire-balling southpaw of Cleveland. Peterson left with a lead after throwing seven-plus innings. Broadcaster and good guy Herb Score told me to run down to the clubhouse door and tell the attendant he wanted Peterson for his post-game show. On the way back up to the press box I ran into Rizzuto, whose night was done. Phil seldom, if ever, stayed for an entire game once his broadcasting duties were over after six innings. He was a very nice man, but I caught him perhaps on a bad night. He mistook me for a Cleveland public relations assistant and said, "Hey kid, do me a favor, call me a cab." To steal comedian Henny Youngman's line, I responded, "Ok, Mr. Rizzuto, you're a cab." Humor may not be my strong point and Rizzuto was a bit flustered with my witty, quick comeback line. Seconds later Rizzuto had a good laugh and off he went.

Working for Pete Franklin was an experience and then some. Known for his bombastic and opinionated on-air delivery, off the air Pete was kind, considerate, and very helpful to me until his death in 2004. Not only was Pete unique, but very few stations during that era devoted an entire talk show to sports. With its booming 50-thousand-watt clear channel signal reaching "38 states and half of Canada" as Pete would often say, Franklin was must-listen radio. Following games I'd call directly into various stadium switchboards, and in those days the operator would put me straight to the manager's office or the clubhouse. Think that would happen today?

June 18, 1975, Fred Lynn, a Red Sox rookie, drove in 10 runs at Detroit. I called Tiger Stadium and got Lynn out of the shower, and he gave Pete a one-on-one exclusive. Nolan Ryan was scratched from a start; I called the Angels clubhouse and spoke to manager Dick Williams, who gave me an answer. Mike Schmidt was the talk of baseball, as was Reggie Jackson, and I had no fear about calling them. Worst case scenario they would say no. They didn't. Pete had a reputation and a huge following.

July 19, 1974, at Cleveland Stadium. It was a hot, muggy night. The following day NBC would roll out their cameras for the "Game of the Week." During Friday's game I sat in the press box next to the legendary Joe Garagiola, who was doing his prep work for Saturday's game featuring the Oakland A's. Garagiola at the time was a top-tier "A" list on-air personality calling national games with Tony Kubek. As the game went on, the drama started to mount. Cleveland's 30-year-old veteran right-hander, Dick Bosman, was flirting with a no-hitter. The A's went down in order in the ninth inning with Bill North striking out to end the game. I convinced Garagiola to come to the station to appear on Pete's show, and he agreed to do so only if I gave him a ride back to the hotel, which I did. In a taxi ride to the station Garagiola shocked me when he told me that was the first time he'd ever seen a no-hitter. All his years of playing, broadcasting, or just hanging out at a park and this was his first no-no? Yep.

Writers would pass through Cleveland promoting their books, Roger Angell and Jerome Holtzman among others. Holtzman had a Hall of Fame career as a writer for several newspapers in Chicago but also penned one of my favorite books of all time, No Cheering in the Press Box, which chronicled the lives of outstanding sports journalists of the era. Holtzman was not only a fantastic writer who knew everyone in baseball, and I mean everyone, but would also share his wisdom with young aspiring students and media members. He was a tremendous man.

Nearing the end of my college education, Ohio University's baseball program held a fundraiser with the help from former school President Vernon Alden. Alden had business ties with Willie Mays. Yes, THAT Willie Mays. We were able to secure perhaps the greatest player to ever put on a baseball uniform to come to Athens, Ohio. Mays had just retired and was open for business as a public speaker. I'm not sure how many school-owned planes the university had, but it was determined that a three-seater would pick up Willie in Columbus, Ohio (75 miles from the school), fly to Athens, and upon arrival we'd take him to lunch prior to the event.

I was selected to be the point person and organize everything. I met the pilot at the school's airport facility. Once I got inside the plane, I thought to myself, "This is barely big enough for me; how in the world is Willie Mays going to squeeze in here?" The weather was starting to change with gusty winds expected, but we experienced little turbulence on the way to Columbus. The pilot landed the plane and accompanied me to the gate as we awaited the arrival of Mays' commercial flight. Mays departed the plane without bags. We introduced ourselves and told him we were going to fly him to Athens. With little fanfare, other than a few autograph seekers, Mays made his way to the private plane terminal and saw the plane he was about to board. He wanted nothing to do with it. Nothing.

I told him it was a quick 15-20 minute flight instead of 90 minutes by car. He reluctantly crawled in, leaving zero room to stretch our legs. The plane took off and within five minutes we hit turbulence, and I'm talking major turbulence. Willie was sweating and I'm thinking to myself, "I can't believe this is how it's going to end. Me, a school pilot, and Willie Mays."

Fortunately, we landed. He was not a happy camper. Can you blame him? At lunch, he ordered the most expensive steak in the restaurant, was not up for small talk, and away we went to the event. He spoke midafternoon for 30-40 minutes and made sure we drove him to Columbus for a flight that night.

My decision to attend Ohio University was one of the best I ever made. I received an outstanding education along with practical experience of broadcasting high school and college athletics. I am so appreciative of the professors and my WOUB colleagues for their support and assistance during my three-plus years on campus. I lived at the station 24-7. I am a proud graduate.

CHAPTER 5
PERSEVERANCE

A few months prior to graduation I began sending tapes and resumes to small and medium-size markets throughout the country. Remember, no internet, cell phones, or social media in 1976. I was prepared to go anywhere. Every week I would go to the library and seek out Broadcast Magazine, which was the only known publication posting job opportunities. I challenged myself that I would send out at least 25 resumes per day. It's called grinding.

With help from engineers at WWWE Radio that I befriended during my internship, I was able to make duplicate copies of my air checks. The process was most difficult; a few nibbles, a lot of rejections, and many stations simply didn't respond. To save money, I took on two jobs unrelated to the radio-TV business. I worked at a sporting goods store 10-6 Monday-Friday and pumped gas at a station a few miles away from my grandparents, midnight to 6 a.m., four nights a week.

In the meantime, I continued to send tapes and resumes to any and all stations. I heard of an internship opening at WERE

Radio in Cleveland, and because of my contacts in the city and familiarity with the market, I got the job. The position entailed news gathering, collecting sports audio clips, and some on-air work and on-site coverage of events.

Before my internship ended, I broke perhaps the biggest story of my career. On Saturday, June 18, 1977, I was at a party and was introduced to a few people, one of whom had family connections with the Cleveland Indians (Guardians) front office, and a big story was about to happen. Manager Frank Robinson, who just two years earlier became the first Black manager in baseball history, was going to be fired the next day. I'm thinking to myself, wait a second, I meet a stranger at a party who gives me a tip on a blockbuster story, now what?

Today it would have been all over Twitter. I called Pete Franklin, who was always in the loop. He told me, and these were his exact words, "Kid, go for it. That's all I'm going to say." In the moment, my heart was pounding, full of excitement, anxiety, and uncertainty. What happens if this story blows up in my face? I'm done forever, I'll never get another job. I decided to go for it. I called WERE at 11 p.m. and went on the air that Frank Robinson will be fired prior to the Indians-Tigers game.

Both the Associated Press and United Press International picked up the story. Only one Cleveland newspaper printed on Sunday: The Cleveland Plain Dealer. The paper's baseball beat reporter was Russ Schneider, a bulldog of a reporter who was tenacious and relentless in every aspect of his profession. With Robinson's story spreading throughout the country I had no idea what was in store for me. WERE Radio passed along messages from just about everyone, ranging from Lou Boda of ABC Radio to Win Elliott of CBS Radio, etc. My career, just getting underway, was on the line, no question about it. I ran to the drugstore at 6 a.m. Sunday to grab the Plain Dealer just to make sure they had not scooped me. Nothing in the paper. It was me, 23 years old against the baseball media establishment. With the Indians and Tigers ready to play at 1 o'clock, the team announced an early morning press conference. Were they going to deny the story? Was Indians GM Phil Seghi, whom I admired very much, going to give Robinson a vote of confidence? Or was Robinson indeed dismissed?

The moment of truth awaited. The press room was jammed full of reporters, cameras, and a few television stations ready to go live as Seghi walked into the room with Senior VP Bob Quinn and Jeff Torborg. Seghi announced that Robinson had been relieved of his duties and Torborg would take over immediately. After the press conference neither Seghi nor Quinn spoke to me. A few media folks congratulated me, but I must admit it was a nerve-racking 16 hours of my life.

Following my WERE run I returned home to Seattle. I love Seattle, and growing up in the Pacific Northwest was awesome. I don't even mind the rain. I did complain about it once when we first moved there and of course my mom offered her wisdom, "Never allow the weather to dictate your attitude." True.

Without a job, I was ready to enroll in graduate school at the University of Washington. Was it my first choice? No. But I needed a Plan B in the event broadcasting was not meant to be. A week before classes began, I received a call from Pete Gross, Sports Director at KIRO Radio in Seattle. He had found a resume that I had sent well over a year earlier with hopes of employment at the station. The position available was basically a glorified paid internship with production work, producing Wayne Cody's sports talk show and some, I repeat, some on-air work. The pay was practically nothing. I didn't care. I needed a job and one in broadcasting to keep my dreams and hopes alive of one day calling NBA basketball.

I loved my time at KIRO. The news-talk station was extremely well-run. We had exceptional talent anchored by our morning drive host Bill Yeend, who is one of the best people / communicators on the planet. Seattle listeners trusted Bill.

Pete Gross was THE premier sportscaster in Seattle. He was a great mentor, advisor, and confidant. He passed away in 1992 at 55. Pete was incredibly important to me and taught me the value of perseverance and mental strength to overcome disappointment, which happens frequently in our business.

In 1978 the station acquired the rights to the Seattle Sonics and Pete was going to replace the popular Bob Blackburn as play-by-play announcer. The plan was for me to step in and become a full-time sports department employee. But Blackburn had strong ties to the community and eventually kept his job. Good for him, not so good for me.

Talk show host Wayne Cody was a showman rather than a sportscaster. He had very limited knowledge of sports but danced around things as well as anyone I've ever met. He could adlib and did it with flair. When Wayne didn't know an answer to a question or lacked sports knowledge, he would hit the mute button and ask me for the correct information and sound like a well-informed host. As a team player it didn't bother me. It was my job to produce and assist Wayne. I totally bought in.

I covered the Sonics for two seasons, going into their home locker room, grabbing those 20-second sound bites for use in morning drive. Jack Sikma, Wally Walker, Paul Silas, Joe Hassett, Dennis Johnson, and Gus Williams were among my favorites. Sikma and I became close friends and I was thrilled he was inducted into the Naismith Hall of Fame.

I was at game seven of the 1978 Finals as the Sonics were

looking for their first title against the Washington Bullets. The Sonics started the season 5-17 and replaced Head Coach Bob Hopkins with Lenny Wilkens, the team's front office executive and a former player-coach for the Sonics. Sikma was inserted into the starting lineup and the team took off. Game seven tipped off at 6 p.m. Seattle time and was tape delayed on CBS. NBA ratings were a disaster and the league's image wasn't good. (Fortunately, Magic Johnson and Larry Bird arrived to save the league in 1979.) I had a great view of game seven sitting near the Washington bench.

The Bullets shocked the Sonics winning game seven on the road. Not an easy task for any team. I made my way to the Bullets locker room to interview Wes Unseld, Elvin Hayes, Bobby Dandridge, and Mitch Kupchak. By the time I arrived in the Sonics locker room many players had already left, a few had not. You could have heard a pin drop. It was silent. No post-game party. No team dinner. Just a bunch of towels on the floor. I was disappointed for Sikma and others, but the Sonics revenged their Finals loss, beating the same Washington ball club the following season in five games to claim their first and only championship.

By the way, the Sonics PR Director was none other than Rick Welts, who later played a vital role assisting Commissioner David Stern by creating and developing All-Star Weekend. Welts had a brilliant career capping off a spectacular run as President of the Golden State Warriors. A few years ago he was inducted into the Basketball Hall of Fame.

Seattle welcomed an NFL expansion team in 1975, and fans in the Pacific Northwest loved them. Who cares if the Hawks were playing the fourth string left guard cut loose by three other teams, it was the NFL! On game day my job for KIRO Radio was to get audio post-game sound bites from players and coaches.

I attacked the responsibility with plenty of enthusiasm and gusto and got to know Seahawks players, coaches, and management on a first name basis. The team's General Manger was John Thompson. Without question he was one of the finest people I've ever met on the planet. Thompson treated me as if I worked at a major network. I will never forget his kindness. Quarterback Jim Zorn and receiver Steve Largent were about to take their games to the next level. They were close on and off the field. Their faith in God formed a strong bond between them, and what they accomplished on the field and in the Seattle community is still being felt today. The two personified class.

The head coach was Jack Patera, an old-school football man with little personality, or at least he was very guarded with members of the media around. He once asked me if I weren't a sportscaster, what would I like to do. I told him I wanted to be the next Elton John. He responded, "Elton John? Who does he play for?" He was kidding. I think. Patera got the most out of his team and I respected him a great deal.

The Seattle Mariners was an expansion team in that era headed by Lou Gorman, another individual who was a terrific asset to young people. June 15 was a key date back in the day as it marked the trade deadline for MLB teams. Honest story. The night of June 15, 1978, I was on the phone from KIRO Radio to Gorman's office. The Mariners played the Yankees that night in New York, and Gorman was waiting for baseball news at his office at the Kingdome while making calls on another line. Again, times were different than in today's Twitter world. When the Associated Press and United Press International would carry news of a baseball transaction, Gorman received it within 30 seconds, courtesy of yours truly. Lou was a wonderful gentleman who went on to have great success with the Red Sox.

I also covered University of Washington athletics. Football coach Don James was great to me, along with his wife Carol. I was familiar with Don and Washington Athletic Director Mike Lude from their days at Kent State University in the Mid-American Conference. When I was a student at Ohio University, I interviewed Coach James several times, so we had a terrific starting point when I arrived in Seattle. Lude was extremely outgoing and such a people person. Washington's basketball coach was a true legend in Marv Harshman, one of the game's great gentlemen.

I try not to look back on my career and play the "I wonder?" game, but it would have been interesting to see where my career would have taken me had I stayed in Seattle.

CHAPTER 6
BACK TO THE MIDWEST

After two years in Seattle, I secured a position as sports talk host at WBNS in Columbus in February 1979. Finally, after internships and spotty on-air opportunities, my time had finally arrived. It was a blast. I was back in my Midwest roots talking Big 10, Cleveland, and Cincinnati sports.

When the Columbus Clippers of the International League played a home game, play-by-play announcer John Gordon would allow me to sit in the booth with him and read scores and add a comment or two. I knew my place. I respected John as a man and broadcaster. John was born in the Detroit area and had ties with a very close and dear friend, Tigers broadcaster Ernie Harwell, so we had that in common, which was a great starting point. The talk show was doing very well, ratings were terrific, and life was good.

In late July, completely out of nowhere, I received a call 15 minutes before we hit the air. It was from a broadcast consultant group requesting an unedited aircheck from that night's show. A position was open at an unnamed major market outlet. I thought it was a joke—a setup by a friend—so I hung up. The consultant called back moments later and explained this was legit and that if I hung up again my name would be withdrawn from consideration. I was a bit nervous after the call, and it affected me quite a bit on the air. Would I be too opinionated? Too vanilla? Will they like my presentation? My interviewing technique? Are the callers compelling? That night we were talking baseball and of course Ohio State football. I didn't feel good about the show, and my engineer was puzzled why we were taping the entire program on several cassettes. Nonetheless, I sent a package to the consultant and waited. A week passed without hearing back so I assumed it was over. It wasn't.

Remember, I was happy in Columbus. Loved the station. Loved our management team and we had a solid following. I was invited to meet John Watkins, Program and News Director at WCFL in Chicago. One small issue…when would I be able to get off work to fly to Chicago for a job interview?

I caught a break. The Big 10 preseason football meetings were to be held in downtown Chicago at the Palmer House. My master plan went to work. I would interview Big 10 coaches and players in the morning, skip lunch, meet with WCFL management at noon, and return to interview more coaches and players until the end of media day at 3 p.m.. I would catch a 4 o'clock flight back to Columbus and be on the air at 7 p.m. Perfect!

Everything fell into place. I took the elevator at Marina Towers to the top of their office on the 16th floor. My heart was racing. This was Chicago. WCFL was in the process of a major format change from rock and roll, a staple of "Super CFL" for decades, to news/talk under an owned and operated broadcast group. The Mutual Broadcasting System was known for their national newscasts, Notre Dame football, and The Larry King Show. I had no idea what I was about to walk in to. Watkins was a high-energy, no-nonsense program manager. The interview went 15 minutes. Tops. I thanked him for his time. He said he would interview other candidates and would let me know within a few days.

On August 14, 1979, I received a call from Watkins offering me the job for $25,000 a year. I was earning $15,000 in Columbus. With the cost of living increase I probably ended up losing money, but how can you turn down Chicago? They would not pay moving expenditures and as I later found out did not pay for my hotel while I was searching for an apartment.

They told me if I wanted the job I had to be in Chicago for an August 20, 8 a.m. meeting. Normally when an employee gives notice it's common courtesy that the window is two weeks. In this case it was all of six days. Seriously? Fortunately, the good folks at WBNS understood and I was off to Chicago.

Highlights in Columbus? I met Woody Hayes and he was, well, Woody Hayes. He had recently been fired after punching Clemson linebacker Charlie Bauman in the Gator Bowl December 29, 1978. The punch cost Hayes his job.

Working with John Gordon was a wonderful experience as he opened his home to me on more than one occasion. He's just a fabulous family man in addition to his Hall of Fame-worthy career with the Minnesota Twins.

I had a chance to see Yankees catcher Thurman Munson weeks prior to his death when the Yankees came to town to play the Columbus Clippers (their Triple-A team) in an afternoon exhibition game. Billy Martin had just replaced Bob Lemon as manager. The plan was for Munson to make a brief appearance and call it a day, which he did.

The manager of the Columbus Clippers was Gene Michael.

(The same Gene Michael that would manage the Chicago Cubs in 1986 and '87.) On August 2, 1979, while working in the newsroom at WBNS, an ABC bulletin rang out announcing the death of Munson, who perished in a plane crash. I knew Michael and Munson were close friends. Michael was visibly shaken, and I gave him plenty of time and space to collect his thoughts before he released a statement.

During the season Yankees owner George Steinbrenner spoiled Columbus fans promoting his organization by having Yankees greats such as Mickey Mantle, White Ford, and Martin make promotional appearances. It was my job to escort them from a suite to the broadcast booth. Here I am, 25 years old, walking down the concourse with Mickey Mantle. A few years back it was Willie Mays. Now, Mickey Mantle.

I also met a lifelong go-to guy in Tim Krass, who passed away in 2022. We had so many good times together. RIP, my friend.

Columbus was also the city that gifted me wisdom from a blues singer, Dick Mackey, that I will never forget. I attended a Mackey show with friends and after a set he came over to the table to talk, and he told me, "You better take care of your homework...if you don't somebody will."

It has resonated throughout my heart for four decades. It is so true. Keep striving for greatness and never assume.

CHAPTER 7
ON TO CHICAGO WCFL

I said "Goodbye, Columbus; Hello, Chicago!" Back in those days there was no such thing as GPS. I booked a room downtown (believing of course the station would pay for it—which it did not). Entering the city I got totally confused. I saw a sign that I thought would take me to the InterContinental Hotel. I was on Lower Wacker Drive and yet I couldn't navigate my way to Michigan Avenue. It was a Sunday in August, a beautiful day. I expected traffic, but I was driving in circles being blocked off by police officers and gates preventing me from getting to my ultimate destination.

I pulled over to the side, rolled down my window and said, "Officer, I'm trying to get to the InterContinental Hotel. How do I get there?" He responded, "I have no idea. Number one, I'm not an officer. Number two, I'm an extra for a movie we're filming called The Blues Brothers." As the late, great radio host Paul Harvey would say, "Now you know the rest of the story."

Our first WCFL meeting took place in a conference room at Marina Towers August 20, 1979. I didn't know one person. Not one. I was the rookie being brought up from Triple-A Columbus. Other than four hours attending the Big 10 media day a month prior, I had no clue what Chicago was all about. I was in awe of its architecture and the enormity of the city itself. It was love at first sight.

Leading the meeting were executives of the Mutual Broadcasting System and WCFL's new General Manager Orrin McDaniels. I liked McDaniels. He was a really good man and didn't meddle at all. I did have immediate concerns, however, when station management said they were ready to overtake WGN, WBBM, and WIND, three excellent radio stations featuring news/talk formats. Our ratings were 0.0—lowest in Chicago history.

The station and Mutual did throw a fancy meet-and-greet party and I introduced myself to Larry King. We talked sports for a good hour. He would be a frequent guest on my show, which preceded his. There was an immediate connection. He loved sports, especially if you discussed the Brooklyn Dodgers.

But WCFL's upper management wanted sports talk to stray from the four major sports to change subject matter every 12 minutes to include topics such as hunting, billiards, ping pong, etc. Excuse me? We're on 7-11 p.m. in the best sports city in the world and you want me talking Ducks Unlimited? (Nothing against ducks, of course, and the organization, but you get my vibe).

We had one week to get ready for our inaugural show and, one other thing I should mention, I didn't have a producer. I was my own producer and I also learned I would be anchoring afternoon drive sports without additional pay. So let me get this straight. I'm anchoring p.m. drive, hosting a four-hour show, producing and booking guests as well, and then weeks later also recording news headlines, without extra pay? Welcome to major market radio! (But truthfully, it wasn't about the money. Seriously. I was ecstatic to be on the radio in Chicago.)

I returned to my hotel room and was mentally wiped out after our first run-through. I had tons of reservations. The unknown scared me. Was I up to the challenge? Was I a bit impetuous in leaving Columbus? I grabbed a sandwich and turned on the TV. The White Sox were playing the Brewers. What I heard I couldn't believe. The Sox TV team of Harry Caray and Jimmy Piersall were ripping new Sox manager Tony LaRussa, who had just taken over from Don Kessinger August 3. I had never heard two home team announcers go after their own manager and selected players the way Caray and Piersall did that night. As I learned later, it was a habit of theirs to criticize Sox players and the manager.

They were loved by White Sox fans for their brash and vitriolic style. I had met Harry a few times while I was interning in Cleveland and found him to be a larger-than-life individual. Little did I know I would be working with Harry three years later at WGN Radio. LaRussa was terrific to deal with. He would occasionally come on the show after Sox games were done. Back in the day, baseball games would last 2:20-2:35 in length. Tony would pick up the phone in the clubhouse and call me on the talk show. How cool was that?

The Cubs were another story. I was VERY outspoken about the direction of the franchise led by William Wrigley and GM Bob Kennedy.

With Herman Franks realizing that retirement was better than managing the hapless 1980 Cubs, General Manager Bob

Kennedy hired long-time baseball man Preston Gomez to pilot the ballclub. Gomez was a terrific person and a good manager, but what little talent he had on the roster underachieved and after a 38-52 start he was fired, replaced by coach Joey Amalfitano.

The Cubs fans were fed up with every phase of the operation. You name it: ownership, front office, manager, and players. I heard it every night on my talk show. In July I said on the air something along the lines of, "If you don't like the ballclub, don't go to games, Snub the Cubs."

Next thing I know it picked up steam, drawing national attention. The date was set for August 29. I was interviewed nonstop and quite honestly it was embarrassing. Little did I know what was in store. I never ducked from my responsibility as a sports talk show host. I attended games at Wrigley Field and was on the field early around the clock. Cubs officials were extremely professional despite the presence of a 26-year-old outspoken talk show host. Remember, we were the only game in town when it came to sports talk. Our ratings were moving the nighttime needle.

Two weeks before "Snub the Cubs" was to take place, I received a call from Kennedy's executive assistant Arlene Gill, a wonderful person who was well-respected by everyone in the organization and by the media who covered the team. Gill explained Kennedy wanted to see me as soon as possible.

With the Cubs on the road I made my way to Kennedy's office. My entrance in the poorly lit room brought an animated and profane Kennedy out of his chair, threatening a lawsuit if I continued to seek a boycott of the game, using language I had never heard before. I didn't say one word. Not one. Kennedy lashed out at me for about two minutes and told me in no uncertain terms to leave his office, which I did.

After consulting with WCFL General Manager Orrin

McDaniels, it was decided the "Snub the Cubs" promotion would cease immediately. Some may believe the station caved, but I disagree. It brought out the frustration of Cubs fans to use a platform, a voice, to air their displeasure with the north side team. The Chicago fan base put the Cubs on notice. They were so done with the direction of the team.

I actually admired Bob for his honesty, but a change had to be made. Kennedy resigned as General Manger in May of 1981, replaced by none other than Franks on an interim basis. The Cubs were a mess and quite candidly I did not enjoy their clubhouse at all. Most of the players were rude. On the other hand, night baseball was a good eight to nine years away, so many of the Cubs players would catch a part of my show. Mike Krukow was a guest on more than one occasion and was always as truthful as he could possibly be and always entertaining. He has been a fixture in the Giants booth for decades, which is no surprise to me.

The Tribune Company bought the team for $21 million in 1981. To put things in perspective some 42 years later, Mets pitcher Max Scherzer earns $43,333,000 a year. After the 1981 season the newly minted owners of the Cubs, the Tribune Company, hired Dallas Green as Vice President and General Manager of the franchise.

In September of '79 I saw a copy of Pro Football Weekly in the WCFL newsroom. I loved it. Great writers. Great insight. Love the NFL. I decided to book the publisher Arthur Arkush. I called the paper. The receptionist put me on hold. The next voice I heard on the phone was that of his son, Hub Arkush, who explained his father had recently passed away and he was now the point person for the publication. Hub agreed to be a guest on the show, and I featured him nearly every week. He was great. Whether it was WCFL, the Loop, or WGN (where he became a major on-air talent in the Bears booth) Hub brought instant credibility to the broadcasts.

We also had a few memorable hockey moments on WCFL. The day of his first NHL game I called a young phenom by the name of Wayne Gretzky in his hotel room in Chicago and asked to interview him for 5 minutes, which actually turned in to a robust 15 minutes. No PR go-between. Just me and #99. Simply by picking up the phone and politely asking the hotel operator, who put me right through to "The Great One" for an interview. No chance that happens in today's world. By the way, the Blackhawks spoiled Gretzky's NHL debut 4-2 on October 10, 1979, in front of 10,138 at Chicago Stadium.

WCFL carried the Blackhawks and the Chicago Sting of the NASL. Having had previous soccer experience doing sideline work with the Seattle Sounders, the station showed a great deal of confidence by allowing me to fill in for Sting legendary broadcaster Howard Balson when Howard slid over to TV. My broadcaster partner was Kenny Stern, son of Sting owner Lee Stern. It was a very uncomfortable arrangement. The owner's son in the booth wasn't exactly an unbiased broadcast, and I mentioned that when questioned by a reporter. It was a conflict of interest.

Of course the owner had a few choice words for me during a game in Atlanta while I was on the air, but in my heart, I know I was right. On the other hand, I should not have made my opinions known publicly nor given an interview to a reporter. Stern had every right to be angry. I used poor judgment. We worked through it and remain friends to this day.

The first Chicago sporting event I attended as a member of the media took place August 26, 1979, a doubleheader against the Orioles. I did my best to introduce myself to as many people as I could, but everything that week was a blur. New names and new faces and a new city, tons of anxiety. It was a lot to handle.

I sat in a chair next to Les Grobstein, a popular sportscaster who was freelancing, collecting sound from the locker room after the game. Within 30 seconds of our opening greeting, Les wanted to talk about the Pittsburgh Pirates. That's right, the Pittsburgh Pirates; Willie Stargell, Dave Parker, Omar Moreno, and Bill Madlock were among the players who came up in the conversation. Maybe he was testing my sports knowledge or maybe it was just his personality, but I listened, and he spoke. I became friends with Les and respected his work ethic. I would see him at practically every sporting event I attended. He was a Chicago institution and there will never, ever be another "Grobber."

Les passed away in 2022 and left an indelible mark on all of us in sports media.

After attending a few Sox weekend games, I introduced myself to owner Bill Veeck. I was well acquainted with Veeck's history from afar. Any baseball fan knew of his story as a colorful, passionate man who provided entertainment with flair for thinking outside the box. But this was the first time I ever met him. Since my brain was absorbing everything Chicago had to offer, Veeck asked me of my impressions of the ballpark and the team. I told him that Sox fans liked to drink, a lot in fact, but were passionate about their team. I told him as much as I respected the history of the park, it was in dire need of major repairs, and he needed a new ballpark. I didn't hold back. I also told him with the Pope visiting Chicago in early October he should ask the Vatican if they could arrange for Pope John II to throw out the ceremonial first pitch during the final home stand against the Mariners. He actually liked that idea. Obviously, it didn't happen, but it was sure worth a try!

Veeck told me his name was listed in the Chicago phone directory and sure enough, it was. October 9, 1979, the Associated Press reported the Sox may be on the verge of moving to Colorado with Denver oilman Marvin Davis purchasing the team. I jumped on it immediately. Veeck not only remembered who I was, he told me he would stay on the air (WCFL) as long as needed. He denied the report.

Veeck's efforts to sell to Edward DeBartolo Sr. was also a no-go. Jerry Reinsdorf and Eddie Einhorn swooped in and bought the franchise for $20 million. The end result is that the team remained in Chicago, and fun times were about to happen on the south side.

Bears President Jim Finks became a very trusted friend from day one. He would frequently call and drop me notes of encouragement and even invited me to his office where he introduced me to "Papa Bear" George Halas. In my opinion, Finks remains one of the greatest sports executives this city has ever seen. Without Finks, the Bears don't win the Super Bowl. He was elected to the Pro Football Hall of Fame one year after he died in 1994.

Finks gave me a super tip in 1982 on draft day at 5:30 a.m. outside the side door at Halas Hall. The Colts would take Ohio State quarterback Art Schlichter with the fourth pick and the Bears with the fifth selection would go for BYU QB Jim McMahon. I kept it close to the vest, but when WGN morning man Wally Phillips threw it to me at 6:05 a.m. I went with the breaking news, keeping Finks name out of it, saying I heard from an NFL source it was a done deal. Sitting next to me was WBBM Sports Director Brad "The Professor" Palmer, a seasoned professional in our industry who was also the analyst in the Bears radio booth alongside the extremely talented play-by-play announcer Joe McConnell. Palmer was flustered with my intel. Timing is everything, I guess. (While at WGN Radio I helped negotiate a radio deal with McMahon joining myself and Jack Brickhouse on Monday night for 15 minutes. I never had any problems with McMahon and found him to be respectful.)

Our ratings at WCFL were nonexistent. On my very first broadcast, August 27, 1979, I put out the call-in number a million times. We received two calls: One was a wrong number, and I kept the caller on the line for 20 minutes. The other misdialed for pizza, so of course we got into a discussion about my new best friend, deep dish pizza, something I had never discovered before I came to Chicago. The late, great engineer Ed Murphy got me through many, many, many difficult nights calling in using different voices hoping to generate some action on the phone lines. We played so many Public Service Announcements to fill the void of commercial content. (Ed passed away several years ago and I miss him greatly.)

There was also growing concern about the station's format, its foundation, and whether Mutual Broadcasting was in it for the long haul. As soon as checks were delivered, I would run to the bank to cash it, fearing the station was a floundering old World Hockey Association franchise in disguise. We tossed away thousands of "Change Your Lifestyle" bumper stickers after station management received a message loud and clear from whatever listeners we had that they liked their lifestyle and didn't want someone telling them otherwise.

As I would always say, "You can't con the fans."

Eventually our sports show on WCFL generated positive buzz around the city and I was in a nice groove. Sun Times/Tribune Radio/TV critic Gary Deeb was extremely complimentary of my work, and I am forever grateful to him for recognizing the effort and energy I put into my craft in Chicago. Every TV/Radio general manager, program manager, news, and sports director and thousands of employees in our industry read Deeb daily. He could make or break you with one column. That's how impactful he was in the market. Without Deeb taking a liking to my work, who knows where I would be today. He was that influential. (Robert Feder, who once worked under Deeb, succeeded Deeb as the preeminent Radio/TV critic in the country. He retired in 2022 after 40+ years on the media beat.)

But despite the good press, I remained fearful of Mutual Broadcasting System pulling the plug on the entire operation.

CHAPTER 8
WLUP

With one eye looking to leave WCFL the timing couldn't have been more perfect then to receive an offer from the hottest radio station in the country in 1980, WLUP FM, commonly known as "The Loop." The station played rock and roll music featuring high energy personalities like the outrageous morning show duo of Steve Dahl and Garry Meier, who took radio to a different level, depending on how you define "different."

Dahl drew national attention when his Disco Demolition Night at Comiskey Park ended in a riot. The playing field was so unplayable the Sox had to forfeit the second game of a doubleheader against the Tigers. The station featured some of the best radio music hosts in the country in Sky Daniels, Mitch Michaels, and Patti Haze. News Director Tom Webb was terrific, as was news anchor Buzz Kilman.

General Manager Les Elias told me his plans were for me to anchor morning and afternoon drive sports and eventually host a Sunday night sports talk show. I liked Elias very much, along with his assistant Greg Solk, a rising star in broadcast management. I was leaving a nightly sports talk show, navigating my way to a new world of sports on a rock and roll station. WCFL offered to give me a two year deal, but I declined.

My first shift on "The Loop" took place September 22, 1980. I sat down in a small booth with a glass partition separating myself and the on-air hosts, in this case Dahl and Meier. Honestly, I didn't know what to expect, but it became very apparent from day one that they were not pleased I invaded their space. They would constantly interrupt my sportscasts and at times not give it back as they moved on to other things. In their eyes I was a nuisance. To a certain degree I understood where they were coming from. Steve and Garry were on the verge of overtaking legendary morning man WGN's Wally Phillips for the top spot in morning drive ratings, and suddenly a new voice arrives taking time away from their show.

I kept my head down and continued to report and cover Chicago sports. My Sunday night sports talk show took us to different venues around the city performing live from the "Thirsty Whale" to "Buffoons." We did salute a "Buffoon of the Week" with a box of Lemonhead Candy sent to the recipient.

On Friday, February 13, 1981, following my morning sportscasts, I hung around the station for 30 minutes or so, then grabbed the bus to take me home. To reiterate, this is 1981. No cell phones, Internet, social media. I returned to the station around 2:30 and saw our receptionist trying her best to answer calls at a frenetic pace.

"What is going on?" I asked myself. I'll tell you what was going on: Steve Dahl had been fired by Heftel Broadcasting for "continued assaults on community standards and repeated violations of company policy" (WLUP release).

I was stunned. Meier was offered the opportunity to stay but declined. It was major news in Chicago. Like front page news.

Dahl was a megastar. He was Howard Stern before Howard Stern. Regardless of if you found him to your liking or not, Dahl was a superstar in the industry.

The station of course took a hit in a.m. drive. It was a major challenge as The Loop welcomed a new executive who would later become one of the industry's greatest visionaries in Jimmy de Castro.

In the summer of 1981 I received a call from Brian McIntyre, PR Director of the Chicago Bulls who later went on to become Senior Vice President of Communications for the NBA. The Bulls were in the market for a public address announcer with Tommy Edwards leaving to program a radio station in Boston.

Bulls General Manager Rod Thorn, a fabulous person and executive along with McIntyre, invited me Chicago Stadium to audition for the position. I read a few lines and did a mock players introduction, and a few days later I was offered the job. I was definitely amped. I had done public address work in high school and at the pro level with the Chicago Sting, but this was a completely different level.

In November of 1981, the Bulls entertained the Washington Bullets (now known as the Wizards). Washington's Jeff Ruland introduced himself to me prior to the game and told me one of their players, Charles Davis, had a "religious experience" and had changed his name to "Shazam" Davis. The gullible me took it to heart so when Davis, a reserve rookie out of Vanderbilt, came off the bench I introduced him as "Shazam Davis." He looked over his shoulder and gave me a puzzled look.

A minute or two later after a hoop I'd announce, "Basket by Shazam Davis." As he was running back on defense Davis was none too pleased. During a dead ball he came over to the scorer's table and said in no uncertain terms, "If you call me Shazam one more time, I'm going to Shazam this up your…"

"Your teammate Jeff Ruland told me you had a religious conversion and you changed your name," I explained. We both looked over at the Washington bench and the Bullets players were laughing beyond belief. Got to have fun, right?

Thorn is known as the man who drafted Michael Jordan, but I'm here to tell you had the draft taken place after the 1984 Olympics I think Portland would have selected Jordan even with Clyde Drexler on the Trailblazers roster. Jordan lit up the Summer Games in Los Angeles and I think it would have been too tempting for Portland not to take him. I can tell you that in addition to Jordan, Thorn loved Charles Barkley, who went fifth to Philadelphia. Thorn turned down numerous trade offers for the third pick, including offers from Philadelphia and Dallas.

Jerry Sloan was the Bulls coach, and I absolutely loved his approach to the game. He wanted his team to play hard, fearless, physical, and smart just as he did as a player. Jerry was into the game for a full 48 minutes. I was concerned about his health because he lived and died with every game, as did Doug Collins when he coached the Bulls. After beating the Knicks in a best-of-three series (game three at Chicago Stadium remains the loudest I've ever experienced at a sporting event) only to be swept by Boston in the 1981 playoffs, expectations were high for the 81-82 campaign. But the Bulls struggled, and Thorn replaced Sloan as Head Coach.

I spent two years as public address for the Bulls and got to know the players as people, not guys in a uniform running up and down the court. Jerry Sloan was outstanding. His second stint as a head coach proved to be one of the best runs in NBA history, 23 years at the helm of the Jazz with back-to-back Western Conference titles only to lose to the Bulls twice. I called

Sloan's last game as an NBA coach, February 9, 2011. It was well-known that Sloan and guard Deron Williams were not on the same page. As the story goes, Williams and Sloan got into a heated argument at halftime of the Bulls-Jazz game. Following the game, Sloan had had enough. He quit. He never coached another game.

I would later spend some time with Sloan at the arena in Salt Lake City when the Bulls would make their yearly visit. His health began to fade in 2018 and he passed away in 2020.

During the early 1980s, David Greenwood and Ronnie Lester became good friends. Greenwood you may recall was taken by the Bulls with the second pick in the 1979 draft after the Bulls lost a coin flip with the Lakers, who selected a guy by the name of Magic Johnson. Had the Bulls won the toss and taken Johnson, there would have been no Michael Jordan in Chicago. Then again, who knows how many titles the Bulls would have captured with Magic? My guess is a few but not six.

Lester was a promising player, a Chicago kid from Dunbar High who suffered a knee injury playing for Iowa during the Hawkeyes NCAA run. Nevertheless, Thorn took Lester in the 1980 draft. Unfortunately, Lester never regained his high level of play due to his knee injury. True story: Lester, Greenwood, and I showed up at a Loyola Academy-New Trier game one night to watch Tommy Tonelli, a Bulls ball boy, hoop for Loyola. The fans at New Trier were respectful and never bothered us. Times have changed.

Attendance wasn't very good in the pre-Jordan era. Just before tipoff one night, Greenwood approached the scorer's table at mid-court and told me, "Chuck, you better introduce the crowd, then you can introduce us."

The Bulls hired Paul Westhead to run the show in 1982. Westhead took the Lakers to the 1980 title but fell out of favor with Magic Johnson and got bounced. Westhead's run in Chicago was a quick one and done after a 28-54 record. It was not a good fit. Incidentally, the other finalist for the Bulls job was Mike Fratello, who did a terrific job with the Atlanta Hawks.

I covered the first Jordan threepeat for WGN Radio. I was not in the Bulls inner circle as I was primarily focused on DePaul basketball, Bears pre-half-post shows, Cubs pre-post programming, and calling Northwestern football on TV.

I had a chance to interview Jordan a handful of times one-on-one and he was always professional and smooth. These days, when the Bulls are in Charlotte to play the Hornets, a team he now owns, it's hit and miss if our paths cross. If he's in attendance he will either sit on the bench or in a suite above the media row in the lower bowl. Without question he is the finest basketball player to ever put on shoes. LeBron James is second, but "MJ" is number one. Did you ever hear Jordan tell reporters he was the best player in the game as James has done? No. He didn't need to. He knew it. The world knew it.

But remember that Michael Jordan didn't win a title until Jerry Krause, the architect of the Bulls, put together those title teams with shrewd trades, draft choices, and free agency. He deserves a ton of credit along with the coaches and staff members as well. Krause was never rude or brief with me. I think he respected my knowledge, and I respected the job he had to do. Because I was so close to the college game broadcasting DePaul and Michigan for a combined 18 seasons, Krause would ask my opinion on college players. That was the extent of it. He did a magnificent job with the Bulls, and I only wish he could have been alive to enjoy the special moment of being enshrined into the Hall of Fame.

CHAPTER 9
WGN RADIO

In early January of 1982 I learned I was under consideration for a sports position at WGN Radio. The next thing I knew I was auditioning for a job on a Monday night in late January while still working drive time at The Loop. That would be unheard of today. Weeks later it was a done deal. WLUP General Manager Jimmy de Castro was very kind and gracious and let me out of my contract so I could join WGN Radio.

WGN Program Manager Dan Fabian was an individual I admired from the start. He was creative and thought outside the box. It didn't matter what position you held at the station, Fabian's door was literally and figuratively open. He cared about everyone. We had a great relationship.

My job was to produce and interview guests during a 45-minute show called "Sports Central" hosted by Jack Brickhouse. The show made its debut April 4, 1982. The program detailed the day's top sports stories in Chicago and nationally. Nothing was promised to me regarding a larger profile. In other words I was receiving a one-year audition from America's number one radio station. I took a $4,000 pay cut leaving WLUP, but working at WGN was something I just couldn't pass up at 27 years old.

Working side by side with Brickhouse was a bit intimidating. After all, he was an absolute icon. I was in chapter one of my career, but Jack was great to me, as was his wife, Pat. Even though Jack was no longer calling Cubs baseball, the Tribune Company, for good reason, wanted to maintain a solid relationship with Jack knowing he had thousands of loyal followers who respected and admired him for years. I too admired Jack long before working with him. I respected his joy and passion for baseball, but Jack was so much more than the Cubs. He had anchored Presidential conventions, called World Series, Bears football, and NFL title games. You name it, Jack did it all. He's in the Baseball Hall of Fame and the Radio Hall of Fame.

Jack knew everyone, and I mean everyone. In 1983, the Colts and Broncos engineered a blockbuster deal that sent the rights of QB John Elway to the Broncos. Jack asked me who the Colts GM was, and I told him it was Ernie Accorsi, but it was owner Bob Irsay who really made the deal. Jack pulled out a tattered black book from his sport coat pocket, picked up the phone and called Irsay directly and arranged a 10-minute interview. He did this countless times with so many celebrity sports figures. Jack would arrive to the station 15 minutes before going on the air. He would glance over the script, sit in the lead chair, and get it done. We had so many great talks about life and broadcasting. I worked my tail off on the show, put in some very long hours, and it was a pleasure.

My dedication to WGN Radio paid off as Fabian suggested I join afternoon host Bob Collins for sports updates. Similar to what I went through with Steve Dahl, I sensed Bob did not sign off on the idea of having another voice joining the program. It was a bit rocky at the start, but somehow, we found a common ground as I accepted the role of being someone Bob could playfully joke around with at my expense.

I loved working with Bob, providing entertainment for our audience. Bob was an outstanding communicator and a consistent number one rated host in the market. He had a remarkable connection with his audience. When he took his show on the road, huge crowds would come out to see him. After I left WGN in 1994, we spoke quite a bit, sometimes two or three times a month. When my travels took me to Chicago I would stop by the station and reconnect.

On February 2, 2000, the Raptors were on their way to San Antonio. I was hoping to meet Bob in Milwaukee three days later, but he had other plans. On February 8, 2000, while broadcasting a Raptors-Atlanta Hawks game in Toronto, my cell phone was going off every 15-20 seconds. Our engineer Greg Lowe took a few calls while writing notes. As we took a commercial break. I asked him what was happening. He handed me a note, "Bob Collins has been killed in a plane crash."

I couldn't believe it. I was stunned. I had just a few seconds to collect myself, but throughout the broadcast I kept thinking of his wife Christine, the WGN radio family, and his thousands and thousands of loyal listeners. The fact we had just spoken a few days before made it so raw and surreal.

This is the type of man Bob Collins was. My mom was near death in January of 1987. I received a call from the hospital saying that at best she had one day left. I arrived at WGN Monday at my usual time of 4:30 a.m. I wanted to personally tell Bob I would be out for the foreseeable future. I had a flight to catch and had to leave immediately. Very few people knew my mom was gravely ill. She had battled leukemia for years and was a very private person, and I respected her wishes. Bob pulled out his wallet, took out a ton of cash, and said take what you need. Just like that. He told me "Anything you need" and that he was a phone call away. I told Bob thank you but declined. I appreciated his heart, sincerity, and concern. I think of Bob often and miss him.

I also handled some morning duties with Wally Phillips. Wally was a legend but didn't speak to me during commercial breaks. It was uncomfortable. He wasn't necessarily rude; just reserved. I knew my place and had no problems with it. I respect the job Wally did for decades, whether it was in Chicago or Cincinnati. Wally owned Chicago radio for decades and is on my Mt. Rushmore of Chicago personalities, as is Bob Collins.

Roy Leonard personified class. His interviewing style was refreshing as he made his guests feel comfortable. He interviewed big names and treated each star with respect without fawning over them. I had a blast joining Roy on Saturday mornings with our 10-minute sports update. He was a dedicated family man and loved to travel.

I compare WGN Radio megastars of the 80s and 90s to that of the celebrated 1927 New York Yankees batting lineup of Babe Ruth, Lou Gehrig, and others. It was unbelievable. Think about it. The station featured Wally Phillips, Roy Leonard, Bob Collins, Milt Rosenberg, Eddie Schwartz, Floyd Brown, Mary Dee, Rick Rosenthal, Jack Brickhouse, Harry Caray, Milo Hamilton, Vince Lloyd, Lou Boudreau, Dewayne Staats, Wayne Larrivee, Dick Butkus, Ron Santo, and Ray Meyer. Incredible.

During the 1981-82 college basketball season I began helping out on the DePaul broadcasts. Bill Berg was a WGN Radio host and additionally called Blue Demons hoops and filled in for Cubs broadcasters Vince Lloyd and Lou Boudreau. Berg desperately wanted to call Cubs play-by-play but was bypassed when an opening occurred and left the station to become morning host at WCFL and play-by-play announcer for the Chicago Blitz of the fledgling USFL.

The Blue Demons were a feel-good story in college basketball led by "Coach" Ray Meyer. I loved Coach, and his assistants, son Joey and Jim Molinari, formed an outstanding staff. I immersed myself into the DePaul program. When I came to Chicago in 1979, Seattle Sonics All Star Jack Sikma encouraged me to seek out Molinari when I arrived. The two played together at Illinois Wesleyan under the great Denny Bridges. I became close friends with Jack during my time in Seattle and for a number of years I pleaded to Bulls management to trade for him.

DePaul basketball was on fire, and I got my first taste of college play-by-play as a fill-in for Joe McConnell, Loren Brown, and Dewayne Staats. I handled pre-half-post, then took over full-time play-by-play duties in 1988. I became addicted to basketball play-by-play. This was my calling, my bedrock so to speak as I continued my sports broadcasting journey. My goal remained steadfast, to call NBA basketball.

Coach Ray was as authentic as you could possibly find in a human being. He loved his family and loved basketball. One night while hosting my WCFL sports talk show he called me "Ron" throughout the entire interview. I would ask him a question and he'd respond, "Well, Ron…" I'd come back and say, "This is CHUCK Swirsky. Coach, about your upcoming game against Louisville…" He'd respond, "Ron, the Cardinals are really good." The next day I dropped by Alumni Hall and Coach was so apologetic. Totally get it. No worries. Every media person, whether it was news or sports, wanted to get close to Coach Ray.

He showed his true class in the final game he coached. March 23, 1984. DePaul against Wake Forest in St. Louis in NCAA tournament play. The Blue Demons led by 8 points with 3 minutes to play in regulation time and lost the lead and eventually the game in overtime 73-71. Immediately after yet another heart-wrenching tournament loss, CBS producers whisked Coach Ray away from the bench to do a post-game interview. That's right, the losing coach doing an on-court post-game interview. He was a world class human being.

His son Joey succeeded him as head coach in 1985 and was a really good coach. His heart is in Chicago, but I told him on numerous occasions to put feelers out and see if he could jump to another program. I just got the vibe the athletic department for whatever reason felt they could do better. Joey is now a scout for the Los Angeles Clippers. In my opinion he never received the accolades he should have received as a college coach.

I loved hearing Vince Lloyd and Lou Boudreau call Cubs games on radio. Their chemistry, warmth, and friendship came across beautifully. Both were fantastic people. I admired and respected them a ton. Vince was one of the more underrated broadcasters our city has ever seen. The success of Boudreau's outstanding commentary was that he never second guessed. He first guessed. A batter would come up with men on base and Lou would anticipate or suggest what the batter or pitcher may or may not do. It was an art and Boudreau mastered it as well as anyone in the game.

The Milo Hamilton-Harry Caray clash of the baseball broadcasting titans was extremely uncomfortable and unnerving. I'm putting it mildly. I refused to take sides in this unfortunate chapter of my broadcasting career as I saw how ego, jealousy, and envy can rip apart a broadcast booth. Milo left the Pirates in 1980 to join the Cubs broadcast crew under the impression he would succeed Jack Brickhouse. Jack was all in favor of Milo replacing him in the TV booth, but all that changed when the Tribune Company, looking for a big splash, bought the Cubs from the Wrigley family.

Tribune broadcasting executive Jim Dowdle along with Andy McKenna hammered out a deal that would bring Harry to the north side. Milo was crushed and let everyone around him know it. He was more than perturbed. He was obsessed with criticizing Harry every chance he could. The two had a history in St. Louis which didn't end well, and here they were again, this time in Chicago. The drama played out in front of me. I was not in Harry's camp, nor Milo's. I had a job to do at WGN Radio. Period. In the big picture, Milo was calling nine innings of Cubs baseball every game (six radio, three TV) and he was the play-by-play voice of DePaul and the Bulls. It was not just a good job. It was a GREAT job. Maybe the best in the country. Yet, he was always unhappy. It was very sad because he was an outstanding broadcaster. A Hall of Fame broadcaster. He just couldn't let go of the rope.

On June 23, 1984, the charged-up Cubs looked like a solid threat to do some magical things in October, as they took center stage at Wrigley Field against the St. Louis Cardinals. It was a beautiful day for baseball, and it was the NBC Game of the Week with the iconic Bob Costas calling the game. With WGN TV unable to broadcast the game because of NBC's exclusivity, Harry moved over to radio and was the featured broadcaster for the first three and last three innings with Milo handling the middle three.

The Cubs staged a remarkable comeback after trailing 7-1.

In the bottom of the ninth with the Cubs down 9-8 and former Cub-turned-Cardinal closer Bruce Sutter on the mound, Ryne Sandberg tied it up with a solo blast. It was a vintage Harry Caray call. "There's a drive, it might be..it could be..it is..a Home Run! Holy Cow!"

Harry remained in the radio chair to call extra innings baseball. The Cards grabbed an 11-9 lead in the 10th only to see Sandberg rip a two-run game-tying home run. Incredible drama was unfolding on the north side of Chicago. In the 11th inning the Cubs scored the winning run on an RBI single by Dave Owen. Wrigley Field was rocking and so was Harry. This is what made Harry a terrific baseball broadcaster. He embraced big moments.

There were six of us in the tiny Wrigley Field radio booth that day: Harry and Milo, Vince and Lou, engineer Donnie Albert, and me. After the game Harry wrapped things up, picked up his score book and left the booth. In one sweeping motion with his hand, Milo knocked everything off the table as cups of water went flying in the air. Milo was obviously upset that Harry was behind the microphone for one of the greatest games in Cubs history. There was silence in the booth until Donnie signaled to Milo he was about to go on the air.

One other story. I was in charge of writing a weekly show called "This Week with the Cubs." It was a compilation of audio clips of each Cubs game of the week. Harry would record the 15-minute show a few hours before a Saturday game. I would drop off the script at the front desk of the Ambassador East where he lived. On the road, I would fax the script to his hotel.

It was a routine week as I dropped off the script to be taped by Harry the following day. At 2:30 a.m. Saturday morning I was startled hearing my phone ring. A phone call at 2:30 a.m. is never good. The first thing I thought of was the health of my mom, who had been ill. I jumped out of bed in my small one-bedroom apartment and picked up the phone. It was Harry. He was livid, using language I've never heard before.

I can laugh about it now, but at the time it wasn't amusing. Apparently, I included duplicate copies of Thursday's game script and failed to include Friday's notes. That was on me, but I was still upset at his tone and language. I told Harry I would take care of it immediately, which I did, driving to the station at 3 a.m. followed by a stop to Harry's hotel. I also included a note telling Harry I didn't appreciate his language or the time of the call. I did apologize for not proofreading the script, but that was it.

The next morning I received a call from Dan Fabian that he, along with WGN Radio GM Wayne Vriesman, would meet with Harry and me in the Cubs TV broadcast booth prior to the game. Harry was on the offensive right away. Was I intimidated? What do you think? But in my heart, I knew I was right. I try to treat everyone with respect and dignity, and I expect the same in return. Harry closed out the meeting looking straight at me saying, "Remember kid, I'm whiskey and you're water." Ok, then.

The Harry Caray who broadcast Sox games was 180 degrees different from the Harry Caray with the Cubs. Harry very seldom if at all second-guessed Cub managers or players as he did frequently with the Sox. He was a money maker for the Cubs franchise, WGN, and more importantly for himself. Harry became a glorified cheerleader with the backdrop being WGN's Superstation status. Harry opened the door for Cubs fans to unite everywhere. I admire his passion for baseball and how he related to fans. My relationship with him was strictly professional. I never shared a drink or meal with him and that was fine with me.

Cubs baseball boss Dallas Green appeared weekly on WGN Radio as I hosted his show, and trust me, he brought the heat each and every week. He would be critical of players at times, even second guess his manager, but we had a terrific relationship. It didn't end well for Green, but he made the Cubs relevant in the 80s. I could speak candidly in front of Dallas behind closed doors. He welcomed it. I respected Dallas very, very much. You knew exactly where you stood.

The idea of putting former Cubs manager Jim Frey in the broadcasting booth was a brilliant one engineered by Dan Fabian. Frey was actually decent on the air but offered few opinions on players or front office moves. I wonder why? Frey and the Cubs won the Eastern Division and he was named NL Manager of the Year in 1984, his first season as Cubs manager, but the ball club blew a 2-0 best of five 1984 NLCS lead, and he was released during the 1986 season. I still maintain Frey should have started Rick Sutcliffe in Game Four, but Frey changed his mind. The Padres went on to win game five of the '84 NLCS and a ticket to the World Series.

(Side note: The very same day of the monumental Cubs collapse, October 7, 1984, Walter Payton became the all-time leading rusher in NFL history in the Bears 20-7 win over the Saints at Soldier Field.)

In 1987 Frey was in the booth and one year later became General Manager of the Cubs. Frey was an old-school baseball man through and through. He could talk baseball for hours, and I could listen for hours. I'm surprised he never managed again after his days ended with the Cubs. He was only 55 at the time. Frey was a better manager than General Manager. His moves to acquire Calvin Schiraldi and Goose Gossage were not good. Mitch Williams had a terrific 1989 season, then struggled and was dealt to Philadelphia in 1991. Frey picked up George Bell,

Danny Jackson, and Dave Smith in the free agent market. No thank you. Larry Himes, formerly of the White Sox, ended up replacing Frey as team executive.

In 1988 WGN Radio and the Cubs went looking for a new radio analyst and I was sold on Davey Nelson, who I got to know when he was a first base coach for the White Sox in the mid-1980s. Davey was a bright, articulate, knowledgeable baseball man, and I was convinced he could make a smooth transition to the booth. I had interviewed him many times and he was extremely comfortable in front of a microphone.

Unfortunately, after two years, a change was made as the 1990 season featured not one, not two, but three new Cubs radio voices. With Dewayne Staats leaving to become the new voice of the New York Yankees, WGN Radio/TV began searching for a new Cubs broadcaster. They cast a wide net seeking the next primary radio play-by-play broadcaster. We were inundated with names, and I received hundreds of calls from agents, currently employed MLB broadcasters, and even fans who felt they could get it done in the booth. I was sold on Bob Brenly as any analyst. I was convinced he would be great. I first met Bob when the two of us were freshmen at Ohio University where he starred in the Mid-American Conference and later became a core player on San Francisco Giants teams in the 1980s.

Dan Fabian, once again thinking outside the box, decided to go with a three-man booth, bringing in Bob and Ron Santo, who bled Cubbie blue and wanted the job badly. Next up: play-by-play. Tons of great candidates were available, no shortage whatsoever. The Tribune Company agreed to terms with 26-year-old Thom Brennaman, an incredibly gifted broadcaster from Ohio University. We had three Ohio University graduates connected with Cubs baseball. Brennaman, Brenly, and myself (I continued to host pre- and post-game programming). The booth was insightful, energized, and had chemistry. We also had fun, and when you play 162 games, you better have fun.

In mid-April 1994, Cubs public address announcer Wayne Messmer was shot in the throat outside of a Chicago restaurant. Fortunately, he survived the shooting but required months of therapy and rest. Cubs executive John McDonough called me and offered me the position to be Messmer's fill-in for the season. Having done PA work with the Bulls and Chicago Sting and one preseason Bears game, I jumped at the opportunity. I had a blast. It didn't matter that the strike-shortened season brought their final record to 49-64. I played it straight with the exception of an inning-ending double play by the opposing team where I announced, "And that's a double play!"

My 12-year run at WGN Radio was an amazing experience. In addition to anchoring morning drive sports, hosting Cubs programming, and calling DePaul basketball, I hosted pre-half-post game shows on the Bears radio network. The 1985 Bears were so much fun to deal with, as my frequent trips to Halas Hall taught me to expect the unexpected. The team was nasty, physical, and impactful on the field and just as colorful off it. Whether it was "The Fridge" or the "Punky QB," this team had a spirit about them that captured the hearts of America. It was an absolute pleasure to witness greatness. Unfortunately, they made only one Super Bowl appearance during their mini run. Inconsistency at quarterback, primarily the health of their starting quarterback, came into play.

We had a great broadcast crew featuring the extremely talented play-by-play man Wayne Larrivee along with Bears icon, Hall of Famer Dick Butkus, and Jim Hart, who was an outstanding NFL quarterback for nearly 20 years. In fact, Hart's last season as an NFL quarterback was in 1984 with Washington. He was in the Bears booth the following season.

On September 29, 1985, Washington played the Bears at Soldier Field. Hart, upstairs in the radio booth, picked up the signs from the Washington sideline to the huddle and knew exactly what QB Joe Theismann and his team were running. I'm not talking about every third or fifth play, I'm talking EVERY play. It was crazy.

Butkus is a larger-than-life human being. He was great to deal with and never big-timed me once when he was in the Bears booth. It was a fantastic get by Dan Fabian. Another great get was the coach. Mike Ditka would appear every Monday morning with Bob Collins and yours truly, and credit Ditka for always telling it like it is. It was MUST-listen radio. The players would tune in just for the Ditka segment alone.

Super Bowl XX was an amazing experience in New Orleans. Dave Eanet and Hub Arkush were at every event the NFL and Bears had to offer. Both deserve a ton of credit as they navigated their way through hundreds of media covering the event. The Bears were bigger than life. They were the number one story, not just in sports, but everything. America loved the 1985 Bears.

The Super Bowl week was a spectacle. Bears quarterback Jim McMahon was accused by a New Orleans TV sportscaster of calling New Orleans women "sluts" and New Orleans people "ignorant." The station later apologized for airing false information and the sportscaster in question, Buddy Diliberto, was suspended.

When it was all said and done, the Bears demolished the Patriots 46-10, but after the game I was locked in on Walter Payton. I was expecting "Sweetness" to be joyous, emotional, giddy, celebratory. He wasn't. As he walked off the field, I could sense something was eating at him. He wasn't happy. Having been around the team the entire season I knew right away what was going on. He did not score a touchdown in the biggest game of his career. He was hurt, angry, and ticked off. Instead Ditka gave the ball to "The Fridge" Williams Perry who did cross the goal line from one yard out in the third quarter, sending a sellout crowd of 73,818 into a frenzy. Everyone loved Perry, and while we admired and marveled at Payton's incredible career, in 1985, Perry was THE story in the NFL.

The truth is that we in the media and the fan base had started taking Payton for granted. It wasn't right. Every year Payton should have been the highest paid player in the NFL. Payton was reluctant to do a post-game Super Bowl interview but was talked into going on live with NBC's Bob Costas by Bears Public Relations Director, Ken Valdiserri, who had a great rapport with everyone connected to the franchise. The biggest moment in the history of Chicago sports and your superstar running back was beyond upset. Since then, Ditka has made many public statements that he regrets not getting Payton the ball.

I had a professional relationship with Payton. I seldom interviewed him one-on-one, but when I did, he was always professional and always polite. Defensive Coordinator Buddy Ryan was great to me and always had a "must listen" sound bite, whether it was about his team or the opponent. When he would see me, he would always say, "Chuck, need anything?" How cool is that? Dave Duerson was also an outstanding interview and was pure class. I still can't believe both Payton and Duerson have passed. Buddy is gone too. Life is just too fragile.

In August 1994, I was called in to Dan Fabian's office. By

then he had been promoted to General Manager of the station. At the time I was married with two young children and a third on the way. Dan didn't pull any punches. He was having difficulty securing an extension with DePaul on a new radio rights contract and was about to make a deal with Northwestern to air football and basketball games. Fabian told me Dave Eanet would remain as the Voice of the Cats, which I totally understood and endorsed. Dave is an exceptional broadcaster and a better human being. He is total class, and I am proud to have brought him back to Chicago in 1984 after he left WBBM for Washington DC. He is Northwestern.

My heart was torn, however. I loved WGN Radio. Loved my job. Loved living in Wheaton. Loved sports in Chicago. But my heart and soul told me to chase my life-long dream to become an NBA broadcaster. I was under contract with WGN, but I also knew if a job opened elsewhere, Fabian wouldn't prevent me from leaving. Ten days later, Tigers Hall of Fame broadcaster Ernie Harwell, whom I first met when I was twelve, called and informed me WJR Radio in Detroit had an opening for a sports talk host, play-by-play announcer for Michigan basketball, and pre-half-post game host on the Michigan football network.

I sent a tape and one week later I flew to Detroit interviewing for the position. I thoroughly enjoyed my interview with the station's program manager Phil Boyce. We were on the same page. The big question was leaving my comfort zone in Chicago for a new beginning. I was not offered the job that day in Detroit but felt confident about where this was going. My mind was racing with possibilities and anxiety. My faith is very strong, and I always pray for guidance and direction. I don't pray for things. I pray for God's will. God's plan is perfect even though I may not completely understand things. In my heart, I know He is in control. One week later I gave my notice to WGN Radio, and I was off to Detroit.

I loved my first run in Chicago. Whether it was covering Michael Jordan and three NBA titles, a Bears Super Bowl XX title, Chicago Sting titles, the Blackhawks reaching the Stanley Cup Finals in 1992, the '83 and '93 Sox or the '84 and '89 Cubs, I learned so much about the business.

I thank all the women and men who I worked from 1979-94. You remain appreciated from the bottom of my heart.

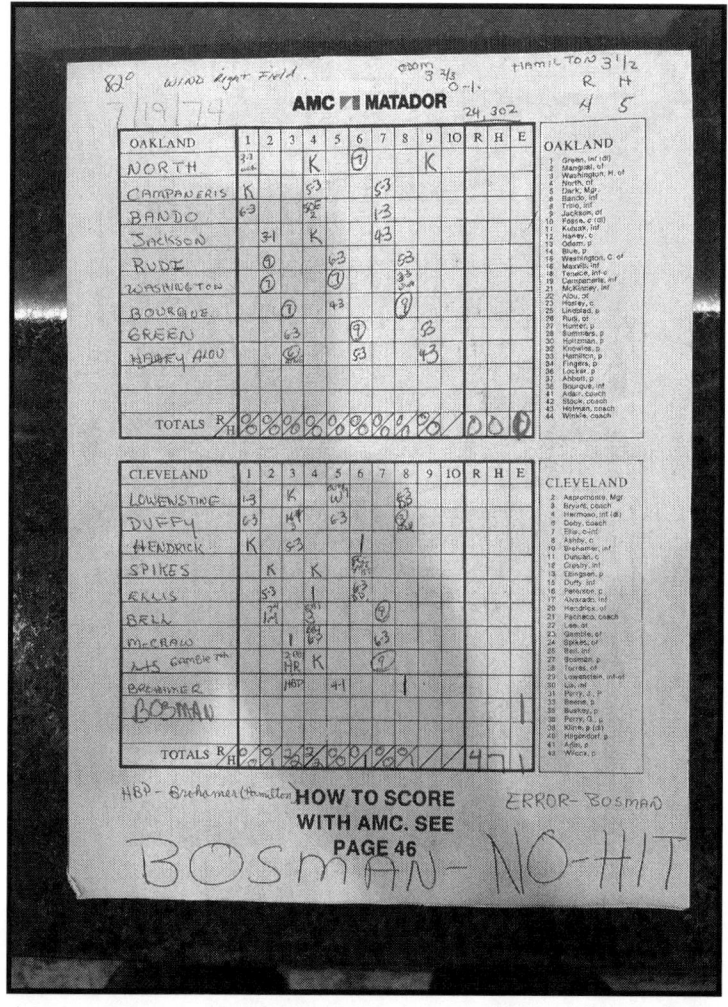

When I attend a baseball game, I very seldom keep score. For whatever reason, on this particular night -The only no hitter I've ever seen live. Cleveland's Dick Bosman threw a no hitter against Oakland. I sat next to Joe Garagiola in Cleveland.

Chuck Swirsky

With Tommy Lasorda and Sparky Anderson

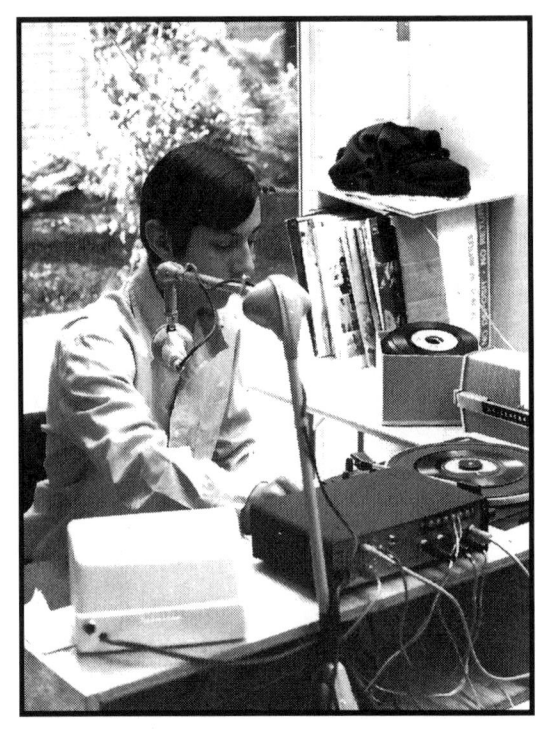

In high school I was an after-school DJ. Notice the vinyl records!

Please help! I engineered my own games at Michigan

At home on the United Center floor

My final WOUB sportscast, March 1976. With degree in hand it was time to find work!

A throwback to my freshman year at Ohio University on WOUB TV interviewing the school's field hockey coach. Quite the fashion statement!

On the Raptors game ticket, back in the day.

I first met Blackhawks icon Eddie Olczyk as a teenager at Brother Rice High School in Chicago. He played 16 seasons in the NHL and won the Stanley Cup with the New York Rangers in 1994. He was the head coach of the Pittsburgh Penguins for two seasons. Eddie and Pat Foley were a remarkable broadcasting team.

Chuck Swirsky

Hockey Hall of Fame goalie Tony Esposito loved talking Bulls basketball. I would see him from time to time at the United Center and he was a true legend.

Bulls press credential. Game 5, Los Angeles.

"The Golden Jet" Bobby Hull was a game changer in so many ways. His blistering shot and flair for the game added so much to the history of the NHL and WHA.

My dad was a man of faith, integrity and character.

Zach LaVine has placed himself among the elite players in the NBA. He signed a five-year deal in the off season and is the face of the Bulls franchise.

With Lou Holtz

Prior to the 1989 season a Cubs Convention panel featured left to right: Don Zimmer, Harry Caray, me, Dewayne Staats, Jack Brickhouse and Dave Nelson. The Cubs won the division but fell to the Giants in the playoffs

With " Cheers" and Saturday Night Live star George Wendt. He was a member of the "Swerski" brothers roundtable discussing "Da Bears" and Chicago sports on SNL.

Family is everything. As a kid I was blessed to have a loving family.

My dad's ship, the USS Sierra (AD-18). I loved the naval base

With all due respect to the 1972 Miami Dolphins, the greatest single season in NFL history belongs to the 1985 Chicago Bears.

Bob Collins left an indelible mark on millions of listeners in the Midwest, and I thoroughly enjoyed my time at WGN radio with him and the entire morning staff.

Another member of the Raptors broadcast team was Leo Rautons who starred at Syracuse and a former first round pick by the 76ers. From Toronto, Leo helped grow the game on and off the court.

I'm offering a few tennis tips to Hall of Famer players Don Budge (L) and Jack Kramer (R).

With former Bradley and Northern Illinois and Western Illinois Head Coach Jim Molinari. "Mol" has been a trusted friend for over forty years and played a key role in DePaul's success in the 1970-80 era.

How I wish he had signed with the Bulls instead of the Heat. Either way, Hall of Fame player Chris Bosh is one of the best people on the planet.

This picture was taken two weeks before calling my first NBA game with my Raptors radio broadcaster partner, Jack Armstrong. Jack is without question one of the best analysts in the NBA going on his 25th season in Toronto

Bill Walton was the finest college basketball player I ever saw in my life. Injuries prevented him from being a top five NBA player but he's in the Hall of Fame leading Portland to their only title in 1977. Bill overcame a speech impediment and is a terrific college basketball TV analyst where there is no such thing as a filter.

The best halftime show I ever recorded came in Portland interviewing the Trail Blazers assistant Video Coordinator, my son, T.C. who is now an assistant coach with the Memphis Hustle of the G-League. I am proud of all of my children regardless of their chosen profession.

"The Chairman" Jerry Reinsdorf is the best sports owner in Chicago history. More importantly, it's how he treats and values his employees that really matters. I love the man. His heart, legacy and generosity for Chicagoland charities will be felt for generations to come.

Nobody loves and cares more about the Bulls than John Paxson. Whether it was on the court or in the office, "Pax" showed up every day trying to improve the Bulls. He's a man of integrity and character.

As play by play announcer for the University of Michigan basketball program, games against Michigan State were very intense. Sometimes it carried off to court matters as well. When it is all said and done, Tom Izzo will go down as one of the top ten college coaches of all time.

One of the best basketball minds I have ever been around, Doug Collins.

Marv Albert set the standard for all of us who call NBA games. A legend.

Without the presence of Joe Tait in my world there is no way I would be an NBA broadcaster. I met Joe nearly 50 years ago and without his support, assistance and wisdom I'm not sure what I'd be doing. He was an extraordinary play by play broadcaster in multiple sports and excelled in each one. He's a member of the Basketball Hall of Fame media wing.

I spent well over a decade calling DePaul University games. Stephen Howard (R) and David Booth (L) provided Blue Demons fans with plenty of excitement in the early 1990s.

The late Craig Sager was gifted in so many ways with his passion and joy serving as sideline reporter for TNT. Craig battled cancer to the very end and taught all of us a lesson of courage, heart and perseverance.

If there is a signature "Voice" in the NBA it has to be the classy Mike Breen. Mike is superb at his craft and consistent in his pace and delivery. A wonderful person who always has time for the NBA fraternity of broadcasters.

Nothing beats calling NBA playoff games. I love the anticipation, tension, pressure and execution of the call and the game.

Always a Pleasure

The first broadcaster that I listened to on a regular basis was Seattle's Bill Schonely who called every sport including the ill-fated Seattle Pilots in their lone season of 1969. Bill went on to become the first play by play announcer of the Portland Trailblazers and coined the popular " Rip City" slogan that remains very much alive in the branding of the franchise.

DeMar DeRozan is good as it gets. His attention to detail is second to none. The Bulls are most fortunate to have him on and off the court. A sure-fire Hall of Fame player.

Jason Benetti is already a superstar and before it's all over will call countless World Series games and have a place in the Baseball Hall of Fame. What a talent!

One of the most memorable games I ever called came in Atlanta on March 1, 2019, as the Bulls beat the Hawks 168-161 in 4 overtimes. I was actually hoping for an NBA record fifth. True. Don't believe me? Ask, Bill. I was so amped I didn't sleep for an entire day.

I'll gladly trade places with Jimmy Butler on the 1st and 15th of each month!

My prediction for the outstanding Adam Amin: He will call multiple Super Bowl games. Adam is a fabulous broadcaster.

If you don't love Joakim Noah, something is wrong. He's got a pure heart and soul. Period. He left it on the court each and every night.

"Coach Thibs" taught me plenty about the game of basketball. Every pre-game show was a clinic.

In the White House standing next to the portrait of one of my favorite United States presidents, John F. Kennedy.

A huge turning point in my life was the day I enrolled at Ohio University. What a fantastic time I had. I grew and matured in ways I thought I'd never achieve.

Chuck Swirsky

A thrill of a lifetime. The late/great Tom Petty sat courtside, two feet from me during a Bulls-Lakers game. I rushed to meet him at halftime. He said, "I could hear you from where we're sitting, keep doing your thing. You're good." What a rush!

Bulls Head Coach Billy Donovan is as good as it gets. Not only is he a gifted coach, more importantly, he's an incredible man.

We love to have fun on the radio. Without the expertise and professionalism of our engineer Rich Wyatt we would be completely lost. Trust me!

Talk about icons! The legendary Al McCoy nearing 90 years young continues to broadcast Suns basketball with energy and passion. Everyone in the Association loves Al!

Chuck Swirsky

Team photo featuring Neil Funk, Stacey King, Bill Wennington and me 2009.

My mom was the greatest influence in my life. A remarkable woman of faith, dignity, class and humility

Always a Pleasure

The incomparable Sue Bird. The Hall of Fame awaits her.

Without any doubt, "The Czar" of 670 The Score. Mitch Rosen is perhaps the greatest sports radio executive this country has ever seen. He has tremendous insight, people skills and passion for the industry.

Chuck Swirsky

There will only be one "Vinsanity." A tremendous talent worthy of the Hall of Fame and the greatest dunker I've ever seen.

Scottie Pippen has become a lightning rod with his harsh opinions on Michael Jordan. My hope is that one day Scottie will reflect on his days with the Bulls and embrace the fact that true championships are built on teamwork, trust and greatness.

One of my all-time favorite people in or outside the game of basketball is Hall of Fame executive, Wayne Embry. His journey as an NBA player and executive is captivating. He became the first African American General Manager in NBA history guiding the Milwaukee Bucks and the Cleveland Cavaliers. Wayne is a senior advisor for the Toronto Raptors.

Fred Hoiberg is one of the nicest men I've met in basketball. He tried his best during his four years as Head Coach of the Bulls and returned to the college game in 2019.

I've been fortunate to be at the White House not once but twice during President Barack Obama's terms. It was an incredible experience to say the least. The President thoroughly enjoyed meeting his hometown team and my 15 seconds with the President was awe inspiring.

Kareem Abdul Jabbar has never received his proper respect as a top three player in the history of the NBA. He's very misunderstood. His reluctance to play the "media game" cost him in so many ways during and after he played.

Tons of expectations for Dwyane Wade when he returned to his hometown but sadly it was a short stay. Nonetheless, he was total class and did a ton giving back to the community.

Other than the fact my tie is too long, I love this picture with Coach Ray Meyer. There will never, ever be another "Coach." What a great, great man.

The world-famous Drake grew up in Toronto and is a huge Raptors fan and loves the NBA. He grew up watching me on TV and is always outgoing and friendly not only to myself but fans across the world.

I was extremely involved starting up Interlake High School's first radio station, KEGR. Pretty clever call letters since the school's logo featured a St. Bernard moniker.

When "Doctor J" makes a house call, you better believe I'm ready and willing to listen!

I was honored in 2016 to be inducted into the Chicagoland Sports Hall of Fame. I covered the great Ryne Sandberg and the Cubs 24-7 and always found him to be classy and accommodating.

I had a solid relationship with Jerry Krause. He would reach out and ask my opinions of college players that I saw as I called play by play for DePaul and Michigan. My heart breaks for his family that Jerry passed away before he was inducted into the Hall of Fame. I'm glad he's in Springfield, Massachusetts but it was long overdue.

Father Greg Sakowicz, Rector at Holy Name Cathedral has been a tremendous support system in my life. He has enriched my world with faith, grace, mercy, advice and wisdom. PS: Father Greg is THE biggest White Sox fan next to Jerry Reinsdorf.

How lucky was I to call Tracy McGrady ("T-Mac to the rack") and Vince Carter in my first two seasons in the NBA? McGrady is a Hall of Fame player and I saw it early in his career.

Mark Cuban has always been forthright and transparent and is a terrific interview.

One of the toughest moments I ever broadcast took place April 28, 2012. Derrick Rose suffered an ACL injury in game one of the opening round playoff series against Philadelphia. My son Mark is standing in front on the right.

Having the opportunity to become a close friend of Jim Durham remains very near and dear to me. As great of a broadcaster Jim was- and he was fantastic, Jim was even a better human being. He is on my "Mt. Rushmore" of all time broadcasters.

Vince Bagli was one of the most respected men and broadcasters I've ever met. He was the "Dean of Baltimore Sports." I stayed with Vince and his family during summers and accompanied him to work and to events daily. Vince was my first mentor in the business and I'm thankful for his willingness to share his knowledge with me. In 2015 Vince was in the broadcast booth in Baltimore as I called an Orioles-White Sox game.

My first NBA broadcast took place 25 seasons ago on February 5, 1999. It was also the first game for Hall of Fame player Paul Pierce of Boston and future Hall of Fame player, Vince Carter.

(Photo courtesy of the NBA)

Without question Steve Stone is the finest baseball analyst in the game today. His ability to communicate the nuances of the sport without talking over the head of the average fan but not to talk down to a baseball purist is a special art form. He is a master and a future Hall of Fame talent.

My most memorable broadcast took place in Los Angeles January 22, 2006. Kobe Bryant scored 81 points at the expense of the Toronto Raptors. I'm still in awe of his performance. I'm sitting in the lower left-hand corner.

(Picture from NBA).

Always a Pleasure

The best high school basketball player I ever saw in person is Clark Kellogg. Kellogg played at St. Joseph High School in Cleveland. I saw his team lose in the state championship game to Columbus East, but Kellogg was magnificent scoring 51 points and grabbing 24 rebounds. He later starred at Ohio State. Knee injuries forced early retirement after being selected eighth overall by Indiana in 1982. Kellogg always brings his "A" game to college basketball broadcasting.

Ian Eagle is without question one of the greatest play-by-play broadcasters in the history of our profession. He is that good.

One of the best sportscasters to ever call a game. The passion and energy of Gus Johnson comes through each and every broadcast.

Larry and Judy Tanenbaum are two of the finest people I have ever met in my life. Larry is the Chairman of the Toronto Raptors and serves as Chairman of the Board of the NBA. Judy is an incredible person, and I am truly blessed to have them in my world. They are beyond fabulous people.

I've had the pleasure of knowing Adam Silver even before he became Commissioner of the NBA. His vision and passion for the game of basketball is a guiding light for generations to come. He is a superb leader.

Hall of Fame center Jack Sikma became one of my closest friends during his early seasons with the Seattle SuperSonics. His Midwest values of humility and kindness never left him during his stardom in the NBA. His patented " reverse pivot" move befuddled players and was nearly unstoppable.

Rob Pelinka became a valuable member of the Michigan basketball program, reaching the Final 4 three times during his Wolverines career. His leadership helped nurture the development of the Fab 5 era in the early 1990s. He later became my broadcaster partner on the Michigan basketball network. His next stop was the sports agency business as he represented many high-profile players including Kobe Bryant. He currently serves as the Vice President of Basketball Operations for the Los Angeles Lakers.

I've had the pleasure of knowing Stephen Curry since he was 12 years young. His father Dell played for the Raptors from 1999-2002. Stephen was knocking down NBA three pointers even back then. He is a wonderful person who happens to be a superstar.

CHAPTER 10
MOTOWN

With two small children and another on the way, it was off to Michigan to call Wolverines basketball, host pre-half-post football shows, and anchor a nightly sports talk show on another booming 50,000 station, WJR Radio, the "Voice of the Great Lakes."

Leaving Chicago for Detroit was very hard, but this was strictly a career move that turned into a love affair with the state of Michigan. On the broadcasting side of things, calling Michigan basketball was a step up from DePaul.

There will never, ever be another Fab 5. It was a perfect storm of incredibly gifted first-year players who brought extraordinary skills, swag, confidence, and an edge to every single game for two years before Chris Webber left after his sophomore season. The Fab 5 made two straight trips to the NCAA title game only to lose to Duke and North Carolina respectively. The Fab 5 changed the culture of college basketball forever.

When I arrived the Wolverines were coming off an "Elite 8" appearance in the NCAA tournament but were losing Jalen

Rose and Juwan Howard to the pros. Only Jimmy King and Ray Jackson were left from the Fab 5 era, but a new freshmen class highlighted by the nation's high school player of the year Jerod Ward from Mississippi, Dallas big man Maceo Boston, and Detroit's Maurice Taylor. All were ready to make a mark of their own in the Big 10. Michigan ball was front and center on the NCAA map and I was most fortunate to be its play-by-play announcer.

A week before my first Michigan basketball broadcast, I met with the engineering department at WJR Radio. Chief technician Ed Buterbaugh and his assistant Tony Butler (both extremely gifted in the area of radio buttons, knobs, and everything else in between) said it was time to go over details of the broadcast equipment I'd be taking with me during home and road Michigan basketball broadcasts. Wait a minute, I thought. Equipment I'd be taking?

The last time I was a one-man show was in college at WOUB and even then, we had an engineer go with us to high school fields to make sure we got on the air. At WGN Radio I never engineered my own basketball broadcast, for that matter, any broadcast. I could only imagine my father looking down from above saying, "Charlie, you should have paid more attention to things other than sports."

The gap between how the station handled Michigan football and Michigan basketball was night and day. Michigan football game day coverage was huge. It was a production times one hundred, every bell and whistle known to mankind went into the broadcast. No expense was spared. For Michigan basketball the announcer was also the engineer!

My head was spinning looking at two large radio mixers along with multiples wires. I could read the tea leaves and it wasn't pretty. My first Michigan broadcast was coming up soon in Hawaii at the Maui Invitational. I had the WJR engineering staff color code the wires so I knew where they should go. It was a game changer. While the pressure of setting up my own equipment in addition to broadcasting the game was a big transition for me, I got through it and about a month into the season it became routine.

The transition from Chicago to Detroit was smoother than I thought as our third child arrived in early 1995. I loved living in the Ann Arbor area (Saline) and appreciated the Michigan athletic department as they were so helpful getting us acclimated to a new environment. Athletic Directors Joe Roberson and Tom Goss were outstanding, as were assistants Keith Molin and the now current Michigan AD Warde Manuel.

One of my broadcast partners was Rob Pelinka, who was attending law school at Michigan after a solid playing career. He later interned and worked under agent Arn Tellem in Los Angeles before branching out and establishing his own player agency firm featuring Kobe Bryant. I am very proud of Rob, who is the General Manager of the Los Angeles Lakers. He is a terrific person and then some.

But as thrilling as it was to be broadcasting Michigan hoops, my first season was a bit deflating. Veterans Jackson and King just didn't mesh with the new freshman class and chemistry was an issue all season long. Following Michigan's first round NCAA loss to Western Kentucky in 1995 I drove straight from Dayton to Detroit to anchor my nightly talk show. Upon arrival I received news that WJR's Phil Boyce, one of the nation's top program directors, had announced his resignation to accept a job at WABC in New York.

I was heartbroken. One of the key reasons I left WGN for

WJR was the intellect and leadership style of Boyce. I could see why WABC wanted him to lead the way in the nation's largest market, but personally I was crushed. We had a chance to go to lunch several days later and he assured me that I was safe, and that General Manager Mike Fezzey was in my corner. Nevertheless, losing Boyce was a blow to our operation. During my four years at WJR we saw two other individuals attempt to fill the void of Boyce and they couldn't even come close.

His loss was closely followed by another. The morning drive host on WJR was broadcasting legend J.P. McCarthy. He owned the city. His style and people-first personality made him beloved by the city of Detroit. He was a superstar. His unexpected death in August 1995 rocked the city, station, and industry. He was a magnificent communicator. He was THE voice of Detroit. He was the greatest interviewer I've ever heard.

Losing Boyce and McCarthy in the same year was a one-two punch.

Calling Michigan games compared to DePaul was a completely different spectrum altogether. DePaul's biggest rivals were Notre Dame and Marquette. The level of intensity was mild at best. At Michigan it was "Us against the world" mentality. Whether it was jealousy of Michigan's high standards of academic/athletic excellence or remnants of the Fab 5 era, opposing fans across Big 10 country despised the maize and blue. I loved it because in essence it's a sign of respect, but venues such as Mackey Arena on the campus of Purdue University would take the building and fan noise to a different level altogether. (The best college arenas in which I ever had the privilege of calling games, in no particular order: Allen Fieldhouse at Kansas University, Cameron Indoor Stadium at Duke University, Wisconsin Field

House, St. John Arena at Ohio State, and Williams Arena on the campus of the University of Minnesota.)

But the worst of the abuse directed at the Wolverines came in our home state. Early in my Michigan career I made an on-air remark about the verbal abuse Michigan State fans were directing at Michigan players. I said on the air something along the lines of, "It's a cesspool of profanity." The papers picked it up and it became a story to the point I received a call from Tom Izzo, who asked to see me when the two teams met again weeks later in Ann Arbor.

Izzo was direct and didn't mince words defending his Spartan student body. His language was colorful to say the least. I totally got it. But it did put a strain on my professional relationship with him until after I left Michigan for the NBA. When I was in Toronto, the Raptors selected one of his players, Mo Peterson, in the first round. During training camp Izzo paid Peterson a visit in Toronto. I was in the practice facility at the time he arrived. We greeted each other and turned the page. Life is too short to carry grudges of any sort. I'm a big Tom Izzo fan. There's a reason he's in the Hall of Fame. He is a winner. Period.

Of course, I was also lucky to be dealing with a great group of coaches in Ann Arbor as well. Michigan Head Coach Steve Fisher was wonderful to deal with on a daily basis. He was down to earth and kind. I never saw him lose his cool. Not once. Assistant coaches Brian Dutcher, Scott Perry, and Jay Smith couldn't have been nicer.

The Michigan basketball program took a major hit in the early morning hours of February 17, 1996. A car driven by Maurice Taylor flipped over, injuring Robert Traylor, who suffered a broken arm, causing him to miss the rest of the season.

Several other players had minor injuries. Also in the car was recruit Mateen Cleaves who was making an on-campus visit. He was the number one rated player in the state of Michigan and was involved in a fierce recruiting battle between Michigan and Michigan State. The aftermath of the rollover led to an NCAA investigation, which revealed major violations inside the Michigan basketball program involving relationships certain athletes had with booster Ed Martin. It was an ugly scandal to say the least.

During the 1998 inaugural men's Big 10 basketball tournament in Chicago I appeared on a sports talk show in Chicago, and I was so thrilled to be back in the city for several days with my family that near the end of the radio interview I got caught up in the moment and said, "It's great to be back in Chicago, the best sports city on the planet."

Even though in my heart I believed that (and I still do), I was in error. I not only embarrassed my station, but it was also a slight to Detroit, a city made up of hard-working, blue-collar men and women who love their city and sports. The audio clip somehow found its way to Detroit's all sports station WDFN. To this day I still don't know how that sound bite made its way from Chicago to Detroit. It doesn't matter. I own it.

I received a call from WJR General Manager Mike Fezzey and program manager Al Mayers, and understandably, both were upset. When I returned to Detroit, I had a meeting with the two and sincerely apologized. It was a life lesson. When I'm wrong, I hold myself accountable. No excuses. I despise excuses.

I loved living in Ann Arbor. I loved discovering the state of Michigan. I was able to build an outstanding sports department with Dan Dickerson (now Voice of the Tigers) and reporter/producer and all-time great guy, Tom Mazawey. It was a period of growth for me and I'm thankful for the time I spent in Michigan.

Without my Michigan experience there is no way I land an NBA job. Zero chance. Michigan athletics put my career on the map. I could have seen myself remain at Michigan for the rest of my career. One catch, however. The station elected to flip the switch and became the rights holder to rival Michigan State, allowing Michigan to be carried elsewhere on the dial. I can tell you had I still been at WJR there is absolutely no way I would have called Spartans games. I was maize and blue all the way. Luckily, the NBA came calling at the right time and took me away before I had to make that choice. More about that story in the next chapter.

I also had a blast being around the program serving as WJR's pre-half-post game anchor. Michigan football is big time. Big time recruits were everywhere. How can you not love the winged helmet and the classic maize and blue uniforms?

I saw Charles Woodson play, and that alone was worth the price of admission for Wolverines fans. He was an outstanding two-way player and came into his own in the 1997 national championship season, winning the Heisman Trophy.

The legend himself, Bo Schembechler, also had an office in the football building named after him. I can still hear him say, "Swirsky, get in here." Bo was always great to me, as was Lloyd Carr, who became the acting head coach in 1995 after Gary Moeller was fired following an arrest for disorderly conduct at a bar in the greater Detroit area. I met with Coach Carr once a week as we had a family tradition with my children making cookies for him and his staff every Friday. I have the utmost respect for Coach Carr, as a man and as a coach.

The first time I had ever heard of Tom Brady was in the off season prior to the 1997 season when Michigan's superb Sports

Information Director Bruce Madej mentioned in passing that, "This kid Brady has a big-time arm." From that point on he was on my radar. Brady's timeline to greatness remains a remarkable story from backup quarterback to sixth round pick to becoming the greatest quarterback of all time.

The 1997 national championship team was a spectacular ballclub that really didn't have any weaknesses. Quarterback Brian Griese was amazing. The defense was nasty, anchored by Woodson who emerged as a two-way superstar. His punt return for a touchdown against Ohio State still brings chills to me with a fabulous play-by-play call by the late, great Frank Beckmann.

With the baseball strike of 1994 carrying over to spring training of 1995, I interviewed Tigers Manager Sparky Anderson on "Sports Wrap," WJR's evening sports talk show. Anderson refused to manage replacement players. He was placed on an unpaid leave of absence in mid-February for not doing so. Our interview became contentious. It was point and counterpoint. I respected his opinion although we disagreed.

Prior to our on-air conversation we had a very good relationship. I first met Sparky when he guided the Reds before he came to manage the Tigers. The Tigers eventually took Anderson back once the strike ended. Anderson managed the '95 season, but then never managed again. He was only 61. Managerial jobs opened up every season, but the only time he came close to getting another job was with the Angels. Unfortunately, it never materialized.

After his managing days, Sparky would return to Detroit often. On one occasion I sat at the head table of a sports banquet next to Anderson and Scotty Bowman, who was with the Red Wings at the time. I didn't say a word and just listened. It was incredible to be around the two of them in a relaxed state. I only wish the conversation would have gone on for a few more hours. It was simply amazing as the two discussed handling egos, the strategy of managing a game, and much more.

I left on good terms with Sparky before he passed away. My only regret is that he didn't get another chance to manage a big-league team. He loved the game, the dugout, and the clubhouse.

One of my first assignments at WJR was to staff Pistons games led by sensational rookie Grant Hill. Having covered the Bulls for many years I knew firsthand how heated and personal the Bulls-Pistons rivalry had become. It was more than intense. This was downright hatred. On the court it was beyond physical, and for NBA fans, it was awesome.

But the Pistons were feeling the wear and tear of playing into late May and June for a number of seasons, and it caught up with them. Isiah Thomas tore his Achilles tendon in his last home game of the 1993-94 season and never played another NBA game. Bill Laimbeer had retired the year before, and Dennis Rodman was a Spur, soon to be Bull. Joe Dumars was still the team leader and a very effective player along with being a class act. But the "Bad Boys" days were over, and it marked a new era of Pistons ball.

Hill didn't disappoint. His game opened up at the NBA level and was smooth and fluid. Allan Houston was emerging as a star but bolted for the Knicks after the 95-96 season. Doug Collins took the reins with the Pistons in 1995 and coached them two and a half seasons. He guided Detroit to 54 wins during the 1996-97 season. He left Detroit with a winning percentage of .579.

Let me say this about Doug Collins. I saw him as a player.

I covered him with the Bulls and Pistons and did play-by-play in the NBA when Collins was the head coach of the Wizards and 76ers. He has one of the finest basketball minds this game has ever seen. I'm convinced if he had stayed with the Bulls, they would have won a championship. We will never know. But when it comes to knowing the game and breaking a game down, Collins is superb. He was an excellent basketball analyst. One of the best ever.

The big story in Detroit during my four years at WJR was Red Wings hockey. What a machine, directed by Scotty Bowman. The Wings were loaded, and there was no one better to lead them than the Captain, Steve Yzerman. Yzerman was the consummate professional athlete. He was so good, yet never put himself above the team.

Motown rocked during hockey season. They loved their Wings, who ended a 42-year drought winning the Stanley Cup beating the Philadelphia Flyers. Six days after winning the Cup, one of the Wings best players, Vladimir Konstantinov, suffered a brain injury after a limousine he was riding in crashed. I was in the newsroom at WJR when we received a tip regarding an accident involving a well-known Wings player. It was a horrible way to end a beautiful week for sports fans in the area. Despite the tragedy, the Wings won back-to-back Cups, taking care of Washington the following season.

I've said it once and I'll say it again, Scotty Bowman is a genius. Detroit was indeed "Hockeytown." Joe Louis Arena rocked. From ownership on down, the Wings did it right.

CHAPTER 11
O' CANADA

In August of 1998, Maury Gostfrand, an exceptional entertainment agent who represents many national and local broadcasters, notified me that not one, but two NBA teams had play-by-play openings. Both the Sacramento Kings and Toronto Raptors were looking to fill vacancies. I was ready to make the jump to the NBA and pursue a lifelong dream of calling professional basketball. I was ready.

I submitted tapes, and after that it's all subjective. Some people may like your work, others may not. It is what it is. The only time I ever took anything personal was while serving an internship in Cleveland, the news director heard my tape and suggested I think about another line of work. He didn't like my voice and thought I'd struggle getting an on-air job. After that brief conversation in his office, I took a break, went outside, and cried like a baby. I was crushed.

After I returned to my grandparents' home later that night, my grandmother told me in no uncertain terms not to allow one opinion to deter me from my goal of becoming a professional broadcaster with designs on calling NBA basketball. She was right. Just like the junior varsity basketball coach who cut me, the news director at a Cleveland radio station made me that much more determined to accomplish my goal of being a professional sportscaster. I am my own worst critic. I beat myself up after a bad game. I am a perfectionist. I have insecurities. When I have a bad broadcast, I can't sleep.

I heard back from both the Kings and Raptors and face-to-face interviews were scheduled. I took a day off from work at WJR and flew to Sacramento and met with the Kings front office and marketing staff. They were great. Total class. The job was to anchor pre-half-post shows on the Kings radio network and handle fill-in play-by-play, roughly 25 games per season when their primary voice (and fantastic human being) Gary Gerould was on assignment covering auto racing for ABC. In addition to Kings work, the position called for play-by-play duties for the WNBA's Monarchs.

The idea of potentially living in Northern California appealed to me. I had never been to the state capital and was impressed with the city. The Kings explained they were interviewing other candidates, which I totally understood as I headed back to Detroit. I also knew I had an upcoming interview in Toronto with the Raptors and rights holder The Fan 590 several days later.

After my WJR morning drive shift I took a four-hour drive on the 401 from Detroit through Windsor to Toronto to meet with The Fan 590, the Raptors' new radio rights holder. I had only been to Toronto once for a NASL Soccer Bowl game. I didn't have a feel for the city whatsoever. I wasn't entirely new to Canada. I had been to the western part of the country numerous times while living in Seattle. My mom would drive three hours north to Vancouver and other times we would take a ferry to Victoria Island. But Toronto isn't Victoria. Toronto is the fourth largest city in North America behind Mexico City, New York, and Los Angeles.

I arrived at the station and was greeted by Program Manager Nelson Millman and General Manager Doug Ackhurst. The interview lasted 45 minutes, and there was something about Millman that I really liked. His passion for radio and sports was infectious. He truly cared about the product he put on the air. Every detail was discussed. We were on the same page. It was a tremendous sit down/get acquainted session. The question was, would he be willing to hire an American for the job?

Days went by before I heard back from the Raptors requesting a second interview, but this one was primarily with Millman. There was an immediate bond, and no matter what the future held with Sacramento, I wanted the Raptors job. The Raptors and Leafs were building a new arena; Toronto had just drafted promising rookie Vince Carter; they had a superb General Manager in Glen Grunwald and an up-and-coming coach in Butch Carter. In addition, the Raptors had solid ownership led by Larry Tanenbaum and superb management in Richard Peddie and Tom Anselmi. I was not offered the job during my second interview. I was told I'd hear back one way or the other in the near future.

I was at peace no matter what the Raptors/The Fan 590 decided. I presented myself
to the best of my abilities, stressing the fact that as a family, we would make a year-round commitment to live in the Toronto area. Three days later I was offered the job. My lifelong personal and professional ambition of becoming an NBA play-by-play announcer was now reality. Did I mention I took a $40,000 pay cut? I went from United States currency to Canadian loonie and toonies. But I was betting on myself to do well, and in the long run hoping it would pay off.

When I first took the job, the NBA and the Players Association were in the middle of a lockout, so things were on hold. I was hanging out in Ann Arbor spending quality time with my young family. I enjoyed that aspect of it, but I wanted to get going. Millman invited me to do some fill-in sports talk/sports anchor work at the station, which I gladly did. I like to stay active and busy. I caught a hockey game at Maple Leaf Gardens and was in awe of the historic building. With the new Air Canada Centre about to open in February of 1999, I wanted to take advantage of enjoying the moment at the Gardens. One of my highlights during my ten years in Toronto was calling a Raptors-Bucks game there on February 9, 1999.

The lockout was finally lifted in late January with the Raptors holding a brief training camp featuring home and road preseason games against Boston. My head was spinning as I tried to acclimate to my new surroundings along with moving my family not just to another state, but to a new country. My wife at the time, Judy, deserved all the credit as she allowed me to focus on my work. I was staying in a hotel downtown and fell in love with the vibe and electricity of the city. I love the heart of Toronto and the pure kindness of Canadians.

My first NBA broadcast of any sort was a preseason game at Toronto's humongous Skydome (capacity 50,000). In the Raptors' first season of 1995-96 they averaged 23,179. In 1993 the Blue Jays drew over four million fans to the park. Winning is the best marketing tool of all time.

Perhaps it was lack of sleep or stress or a combination of both, but I felt a severe cold coming on. I was emotionally and physically exhausted. My broadcast partner was Jack Armstrong, who had done a fine job as head coach at Niagara

University before moving on to the world of broadcasting. Jack was passionate, opinionated, and loved basketball. The moment Millman brought us together there was instant chemistry. It's remained that way for 25 years. I remember calling DePaul-Niagara games where Jack was so animated on the sideline I thought he'd be perfect with an up-and-coming franchise to create excitement. The real excitement, however, came from a brilliant rookie by the name of Vincent Lamar Carter and a 19-year-old second-year player in Tracy McGrady.

My first experience of calling a preseason NBA game in Toronto was a blur, and I was a play behind all night long. The 24 seconds shot clock was new to me in terms of developing pace and I struggled bringing in Jack as I was concerned about missing a basket. I was disappointed with my performance, and I hardly slept that night.

The following day we left for Boston. I had never been on a charter flight in my life. I arrived at the terminal only to be met by two men who took my bags. I then presented my passport to airline officials and boarded the plane. It was unbelievable. The plane had been reconfigured with plenty of wide leather seats with plenty of leg room. We dined with a tablecloth and silverware. It was first class. Jack and I sat in the back of the plane as players made their way to the front. The coaching staff sat in the middle. Coach Butch Carter was great to me, as were his assistants Brian James, Joe Harrington, and Jim Thomas. I had known of Brian and met him maybe once or twice in passing when he coached high school ball in the Chicagoland area and later when he joined Doug Collins' staff in Detroit. He is an excellent coach.

With a quick one-hour flight to Boston we left the morning of the game and checked in to the Harbor Hotel. It was a beautiful hotel, one I had never seen before. I stood amazed at just about everything.

The familiarity of playing the same team twice in a three-day span was helpful and I anticipated a better broadcast. Even though my body was starting to shut down due to a nasty cold, I got through the game and felt better about the basic elements of calling an NBA contest. As I stated before, I am my own worst critic. I invite constructive criticism from all, but trust me, when I have a bad game or screw up a play, I'm the first to know.

Of all teams to open the lockout season of 98-99, you guessed it, the same Boston Celtics! Our third game in a little over a week against Rick Pitino's ballclub. Friday, February 5, 1999. Raptors at Celtics. My first official NBA game. I was pumped, nervous, excited, and had a fever. I was drinking tons of water and spent most of the day in bed. The show must go on. The voice was strong; the body was not. The game itself? The Raptors shot 39% and won. How? They went 30-35 from the foul line. How has the game changed? The Raps took a total of 10 three-pointers the entire night. 10.

It was the NBA debut of two rookies: Toronto's Vince Carter and Boston's Paul Pierce. Carter scored 16 points. Pierce scored 19. Two seasoned veterans also made their Raptors debut. Kevin Willis scored 28 points and pulled down 16 rebounds. Charles Oakley grabbed nine rebounds. Tracy McGrady came off the bench and scored 13 points in 13 minutes. After the game I was so jacked up. My first NBA broadcast! I thought of my parents and my grandmother who were looking down from above knowing just how hard I worked to get to this level.

After the game it was off to Washington D.C. for the tail end of two games in two nights, this one against the Wizards. I took my seat in the back of the plane and once we took off, I saw Kevin Willis headed to the back. After his monster 40-minute game, he lay down on the floor dealing with severe back spasms. Willis noticed how exuberant I was and with a smile told me,

"Chuck, we have 49 games left in like 99 days."

Keeping things in perspective is always a good thing! It was a spectacular first season for Carter, who won Rookie of the Year and dunked on everyone. It was "Vinsanity" at its finest. I coined the nickname "Air Canada Carter" and it caught on. Carter was must-see TV throughout Canada and the United States as interest in the franchise and the game of basketball started to percolate with players like Carter and McGrady leading the way. The Air Canada Centre opened in late February, and it was beautiful. The fans loved watching Carter and the Raps. The Raptors flirted with a possible playoff spot but struggled down the stretch to finish 23-27. I could sense the next season would be special, and it was.

By the time Carter hit his third and final year of his rookie contract, stories in every NBA city began speculating whether he was planning a quick exit to the United States. Canada couldn't get enough of "Vinsanity" and in turn Vince loved the city. He owned Toronto. With McGrady now in Orlando after electing not to play the wing man role to Carter, fans were getting nervous about the health of the franchise. In August of 2001, Carter erased any speculation about jumping to a US franchise by signing a six-year $94 million contract. Those of us deeply rooted in the Raptors organization were overjoyed. Give credit to ownership and management. I also believe fans in Canada, particularly the greater Toronto area, had a lot to do with Carter returning. The Raptors were playing before sellout crowds every night.

Carter became a major superstar in his third season as he and Philadelphia's Allen Iverson had 50-point games in one of the greatest playoff series in NBA history. Prior to the deciding game seven in Philadelphia of the 2001 Eastern Conference semi-finals, Carter elected to attend his graduation ceremonies at the University of North Carolina and fly immediately to the game for a 5:30 tip. It brought on many strong opinions from both points of views throughout the NBA. I turned down at least fifty media requests for interviews. I refused to go there. This was a decision for Vince and Vince alone. The Raptors supported Carter every step of the way, led by Chairman Larry Tanenbaum. Carter finished with 20 points, 7 rebounds, and 9 assists playing a full 48 minutes but missed a game-winning left corner jumper as time expired. It was a tremendous series.

As the seasons passed, and the Raptors began struggling on the court, Carter became frustrated with the direction of the team. He was dealing with nagging knee injuries as well. His agent approached the Raptors requesting a trade. Speculation started to mount that Carter could be on his way out. My guess was New York, but I was wrong.

At dinner one night in Los Angeles new Raptors General Manager Rob Babcock excused himself to take a call from Portland, who had interest in Vince. Ultimately on December 17, 2004, Carter was dealt by the Raptors to the Nets for Eric Williams, Aaron Williams, Alonzo Mourning, and two first round picks.

I first heard of the trade while hosting my daily sports talk show on The Fan 590 from a restaurant in Indianapolis. The story broke midafternoon. Following the game I remember walking to the bus with Chris Bosh and asked him if he was ready to assume leadership of the team. He said he was. He was 20 years young at the time. Mourning was bought out and the trade was completely one-sided as Carter got back on track, missing only

11 games in four seasons with the Nets.

Without question the toughest game I've ever called was Carter's first game back to Toronto in a Nets uniform, April 15, 2005. The crowd was super charged and super intense, full of unflattering signs and profanity. I loved the Raps as much as anyone can love a team. They gave me an opportunity to call NBA games. They were great to me and my family from Chairman Larry Tanenbaum, President Richard Peddie, and VP Tom Anselmi to employees at Maple Leaf Sports and Entertainment. I was disappointed Vince wanted out, but the truth is mentally he had checked out long before the trade. As the story goes, Carter had a change of heart on the eve of the trade announcement but by that time it was too late. An agreement was reached between the Raptors and Nets management led by General Manager Rod Thorn. The same Rod Thorn that drafted Michael Jordan in 1984.

I didn't bury Vince during the broadcast, but I did express disappointment with his decision to leave. It was very painful for Raptors fans to see their home-grown superstar leave the city wearing a different NBA uniform. The organization went through a brick wall for him on and off the court. In his first game back, Carter had 39 points in a 101-90 Nets win. In January of 2006 he nailed a three-pointer with less than a second remaining as the Nets beat the Raps again in Toronto 105-104 (Vince scored 42 points).

My professional relationship with Vince changed after the trade. It became distant. Years later, I wrote a handwritten note of apology while he was playing in Dallas. I expressed sadness that my personal feelings got in the way of professional standards. I'm pleased to see Vince excelling in television. When he was injured, he would join us on air and was superb. He has a very bright future. I wish him and his family nothing but the best. The Hall of Fame awaits him. But let's be perfectly clear about one thing. Regardless of how things ended for Carter in Toronto, Vince Carter put basketball on the map in Toronto and Canada. Period.

September 11, 2001. I was on my way to Pearson Airport in Toronto for a speaking engagement in Columbus, Ohio. I heard on the car radio that a plane had crashed into one of the Twin Towers in New York. My first thought was a tragic accident. Minutes later another bulletin that a second plane had crashed into the other tower. The United States of America was under attack. The airport was in full lockdown, as were the borders. The last thing on my mind was a speaking engagement. I turned my attention to my children and went directly to their school. It was wall-to-wall TV and radio coverage as the world was in disbelief.

Just as I remember the Kennedy assassination in 1963, I will never forget, nor should we ever forget, September 11, 2001. I've been to Ground Zero countless times to honor those who lost their lives and those brave individuals who saved lives. It is a moving experience, and my thoughts and prayers remain connected to the families who continue to feel emotional trauma from that day. My heart and soul cannot measure the respect and admiration I have for first responders and those women and men who assisted in saving lives and those who lost their lives.

Most memorable Raptors game? Believe it or not, it was a game the Raptors lost, not won. January 22, 2006. It was a sleepy Sunday night at Staples Center in Los Angeles. The 14-26 Raptors took on the 21-19 Lakers who were just two games over .500 at home. The Lakers starting lineup featured players such as

Kwame Brown, Chris Mihm, Smush Parker, and a guy you may have heard of—Kobe Bean Bryant.

There were no A-list celebrities at courtside for this one. No Jack Nicholson. No Adam Sandler. No rock stars. The Raptors jumped on the Lakers, leading by as many as 18 points in the third quarter. Then Kobe went to work with a steal and a slam, and he was just getting started. He scored 55 points after halftime. With 18,997 fans in attendance, Bryant's two free throws with 4.2 remaining gave him 81 on the night as the crowd went crazy. He went 28 of 46 from the floor, 7 of 13 from three-point range, and drained 18-20 from the foul line. The Lakers rallied and came away with a 122-104 victory.

I could not believe what I witnessed. Sam Mitchell used different coverages and tried everyone on Bryant, whether it was Jalen Rose, Chris Bosh, Matt Bonner, Mo Peterson, Mike James, you name it. It's the greatest single game performance I've seen personally by an athlete in my 47 years of professional broadcasting.

I was introduced to Kobe by Rob Pelinka (yes, the same Rob Pelinka that was my broadcast partner in Michigan). He was representing Kobe and arranged a pre-game interview when the Raptors visited the Lakers the following season. From that moment on, every time our paths crossed Kobe would stop and hold a brief conversation with me. Kobe was always polite and attentive. He wasn't looking around to see who else was in the room or coming out of the players' tunnel. He was remarkable in many ways.

On January 26, 2020, I was in a museum in Chicago when my phone started going off. I was in disbelief when I started to look at Twitter.

"Kobe Bryant killed in a helicopter crash."

What? No way! There must be a mistake. Fake news.

Erroneous reporting. But the story was true. My heart sank thinking of his daughter who perished along with the seven others who lost their lives. We will never know what Kobe's second chapter in life would have brought, but we had a glimpse of it as he captured an Academy Award for Best Animated Short Film, Dear Basketball. Kobe had incredible talents outside of basketball.

My ten years in Toronto went by quickly. I called games on radio, then simulcast (radio and TV), and then television. I became a Canadian citizen and immersed myself into the Canadian culture. I developed a strong bond with Raptors fans that will never be broken. I will always love Toronto. I will always love Canada. The fans are great. The culture is great. My children were raised in a multicultural environment. I am proud to be a dual citizen.

The front office, coaches, and players who passed through the doors in Toronto treated me respectfully. Vince Carter, Tracy McGrady, Chris Bosh, Alvin Williams, Mo Peterson, Antonio Davis, Jerome Williams, Aaron Williams, Jalen Rose, Matt Bonner, Charles Oakley, Dell Curry, Muggsy Bogues, Kevin Willis, Jose Calderon, TJ Ford, Anthony Parker, and many more, thank you.

I worked with Jack Armstrong and Canadian icon Leo Rautins and team broadcasters Eric Smith and Paul Jones, and they were outstanding. One of the TV carriers, "The Score," featured Adnan Virk now of MLB TV and DAZN. I gave him the nickname "The Baller" because he loved talking hoops. Directors and producers Dan Gladman, Paul Graham, Troy Clara, Jim Marshall, Liana Ward Bristol, and "Jumpin" Johnny Rusin were fabulous. Raptors massage therapist Ray Chow and I formed a strong bond and shared many meals together with security director Bernie Offstein, who left this world way too soon. Former NCAA official, NBA referee consultant, and global businessman Ron Foxcroft, who is based in the Toronto area, became a valued friend, and I relied on his wisdom and trust through some challenging times. Ron developed the Best Whistle in the World and founded a company on innovation. He is a great man.

Head coaches? We had a few during my ten years in Toronto. In addition to Butch Carter, Lenny Wilkens calmed the rough seas when he guided the team for three seasons. Kevin O'Neill and Sam Mitchell brought flair and passion to the franchise. Mitchell was named Coach of the Year in 2007.

While broadcasting Raptors games, visiting players would ask about the city, ownership, and management. I spoke glowingly about all three. I cannot say enough good things about Raptors Chairman Larry Tanenbaum and his wife Judy. They are on another planet in terms of grace, dignity, professionalism and generosity. I love the two of them very, very much. Larry's passion for people and relationship building is something to behold. The world of sports; the culture of sports, needs more Larry Tanenbaums. People love connecting with them as much as they love supporting charitable causes. Judy is a fabulous individual who continues to leave an indelible mark on the city of Toronto with her philanthropic, giving heart. Without Larry Tanenbaum there is no NBA in the market.

In the twilight of his terrific NBA career, the Raptors signed free agent sharp-shooter Dell Curry. Little did I know at the time when Dell brought his sons to the Air Canada Centre hours before a home game, I would be witnessing two future NBA players. Seth and Stephen Curry loved being on the floor attempting NBA three-point shots. I always came away impressed with the two because of their politeness, respect, and manners they had for everyone. It was always, Mr. Swirsky." I was never referred to by my first name. I am thrilled for their success. Before his career is over, Stephen will be a top five player in NBA history. Seth is a remarkable story of perseverance and never giving up after bouncing around early in his NBA career playing in the shadow of his brother. Seth is one of the top shooters in the game today.

I appreciate the Raptors recognizing my passion for the team and the city and in turn valuing me as an employee and as a human being. We had not one but two "Chuck Swirsky Bobblehead Nights."

When the Raptors were closing in on a win, I would shout out, "Get out the salami and cheese, mama; this ballgame is over." Fans would bring signs to the game. Reserve players entering the game at the scorer's table would joke with me about it.

I thought I would be in Toronto the rest of my life, but one call changed everything.

CHAPTER 12
BACK TO THE FUTURE

A week after the Raptors were eliminated from their opening round 2008 playoff series against Orlando, I received a phone call from MLSE Vice President Tom Anselmi informing me the Bulls had called and asked permission to speak to me about a broadcast opening.

I was surprised. The year prior, I received a call from the Seattle SuperSonics about their radio opening, but the franchise had one foot out the door, and with new ownership prepared to relocate to Oklahoma City, I had no desire to uproot my family twice in as many years. Had Seattle approved a new arena, chances are I would have gone back home broadcasting the team I so deeply loved as a kid.

But the Bulls are the Bulls. The history. The tradition. The logo. The brand. The United Center. The city. Before I placed a call to Bulls Vice President Steve Schanwald I had to think long and hard about this life-changing decision. Was the timing in line with our family needs? Was it right for the children? I loved Toronto and Toronto loved me back. We were dealing with a lot of moving parts but eventually we decided to return to Chicago. I appreciate the sacrifice my children made leaving school and neighborhood friends. It was the hardest professional decision I have ever made. I loved MLSE management in Toronto.

But the Bulls have a great ownership and management team as well.

I've known Chairman Jerry Reinsdorf for over 40 years. He is not only a great man but one that cares deeply about the Chicagoland community. He has poured millions of dollars into charitable and city programs throughout the years. I have the utmost respect for Jerry. I love the man. His son Michael, the President of the Bulls, is committed to the same foundational values and commitment on and off the court. Michael is passionate about winning and doing whatever is necessary to provide winning basketball. He's not in it to be just competitive. He wants to win an NBA championship. Michael's wife Nancy does a fabulous job overseeing Chicago Bulls Charities. I attend a ton of events every season, and to see schools flourish and children learning and growing with the resources provided to assist educators is a beautiful thing. I would go through a brick wall for the Reinsdorf family, and I say this without any agenda or self-serving cause. They are terrific.

The Bulls also have a history of some of the finest play-by-play announcers the sport has ever produced. Bob Costas, Jim Durham, Tom Dore, Neil Funk, and Wayne Larrivee provided exciting calls to Bulls Nation over the last 40-50 years. I was humbled the Bulls would bring me back to Chicago to join that list.

With Funk sliding over to TV, my broadcast partner would be three-time NBA champion Bill Wennington. Bill was a tremendous high school player in Long Island and was heavily recruited by all of the top schools. He turned down Coach K

(Mike Krzyzewski) and Duke not once but twice. My history with Bill dates back to the early 1980s when I broadcast DePaul-St. John's games. When he was inducted into the Canadian Basketball Hall of Fame in Toronto, I was the emcee. Bill is an outstanding partner with great insight and a wonderful personality. He comes prepared every game and doesn't bring a sense of entitlement to the broadcast. He is a very, very close friend and I am truly blessed to have him as my broadcast partner.

A full circle of life was about to embark at the United Center with an exciting young 2008-09 team.

The Bulls opened the 2008-09 season with a new head coach in Vinny Del Negro and the number one overall pick in the draft, Chicago's very own Derrick Rose. From game one it was apparent that Rose had the "IT" factor. His athleticism, strength, speed, and ability to get to the rim was a nightmare for opponents. With ball handling speed from base line to base line, Rose was a blur.

The fact he was from Chicago was even more special. Everyone wanted a piece of Rose. He couldn't go anywhere in Chicago. On the road there was a buzz in the building when the Bulls came to town. I'm not saying it was at the Jordan level, but Rose had the potential of making this a very, very special era in Bulls history. He was named Rookie of the Year as the Bulls finished 41-41 and played Boston in the opening round of the playoffs.

I was having so much fun watching Rose, Joakim Noah, Luol Deng, Kirk Hinrich, and Ben Gordon hoop. The Bulls pulled off a major trade in February 2009, acquiring Brad Miller and John Salmons from Sacramento for four players including Drew

Gooden and one of my favorite Bulls, Andres Nocioni. Nocioni was tough, rugged, nasty, and fearless. I was so disappointed he was dealt, but the bottom line is the Bulls became a better team because of the move.

Any general manager worth his weight knows you're going to be criticized no matter what you do or don't do. It's all about separating the heart and the brain and doing what's best for the team. Miller and Salmons were terrific and gave the Bulls added depth.

I was amped for playoff ball. Game One in Boston was a masterpiece with Rose going for 36 points and 11 assists as the Bulls came away with an OT 105-103 victory. The series went the full seven games with Boston prevailing on its home court. Although Rose was generating plenty of attention, it was Joakim Noah who emerged as a player to be reckoned with for seasons to come.

In Game Six, the Bulls trailed by eight, with two minutes remaining in regulation. They rallied and sent the game into overtime. Not just one overtime, three overtimes. It was a fantastic game with the United Center going crazy after Noah came through with a strip, a steal, and a slam as the Bulls won a thriller. I am a huge Joakim Noah fan. I love his heart for people, his transparency, his kindness, his humor, his charitable activities, everything. He's one of the best human beings I have ever met in or out of basketball.

February 26, 2009, was a most unusual day when it came to celebrating a special occasion, yet dampened by the loss of not one but two Bulls legends.

We learned a few days prior to the Bulls-Wizards game in Washington D.C. we would meet the Bulls biggest fan, The

President of the United States, Barack Obama. Meeting a sitting or former President is an incredible honor and experience. It was a first for me. I had been to the White House in 1996 covering Michigan's NCAA " Frozen Four" men's title, but it was Vice President Al Gore not President Clinton who handled the ceremony.

On our way to meet the President, we learned that both Johnny "Red" Kerr, the organization's first coach and recently retired TV analyst and without question, the franchise's number one ambassador, passed away after a lengthy illness. Johnny was a great man who always brought a smile to everyone with his outgoing personality.

We were also informed that former guard turned TV studio analyst Norm Van Lier died unexpectedly. "Stormin' Norman" was a fabulous player and epitomized what Bulls ball of the 1970s was all about: Rugged, physical, feisty and passionate. It was a somber ride to the White House to say the least.

Upon arrival players, staff members and broadcasters were invited to take a tour of the White House as with great anticipation we were about to meet the President. With a huge smile and enthusiasm, the President spoke to our group, shaking hands and greeting everyone individually. He also attended the game. It's a moment in time that will stay with me forever.

After two years under Del Negro, Noah reached a level of All Star status as he blossomed under Head Coach Tom Thibodeau. Coach Thibs was 365, 24-7 hoops. We recorded a three-minute pre-game show before every game, and he loved breaking it down in a manner only Thibodeau could do. You could ask him about the 15th man on the Kings roster and he would tell you if the player could go left off the dribble, if he likes contact, etc. It was a clinic. I would ask a question then would listen. His brain was wired into basketball as no one I've ever seen. But when the interview was over, and the recorder turned off, I saw a different Coach Thibs than you'd see in press conferences or twenty-second sound bites. He has a great sense of humor.

With Rose sidelined with various injuries, Coach Thibs used Noah as a facilitator at the high post, running the offense through him. It was a brilliant move as Noah's game went to the next level on the defensive side. He reaped the benefits of that hard work when he named NBA Defensive Player of the Year in 2014.

Unfortunately, the window of success featuring Rose, Noah, Luol Deng, and Kirk Hinrich was coming to a close.

Every coach has a shelf life, no matter if it's Vinny Del Negro, Tom Thibodeau, Fred Hoiberg, or Jim Boylan. It's the nature of the business. Coaches understand this the moment they sign on the dotted line. Coaching is intoxicating. Teaching and coaching NBA players is the ultimate. It's the highest of highs and losing brings on the lowest of lows. Coaches anguish more over losses than they celebrate wins. Strange but true. It comes with the territory no matter what sport, level, or league.

With the departure of Thibodeau, the Bulls brought in Fred Hoiberg of Iowa State. Fred had been rumored for NBA jobs but had a good thing going at the collegiate level until the Bulls recruited him. Hoiberg had an excellent reputation inside the Bulls organization having played for the Bulls for four seasons. I saw enough Iowa State games on ESPN to appreciate his offensive schemes.

The majority of college coaches fail to make a successful transition into the NBA. More often than not a college coach who makes the jump to an NBA ends up coaching a bad ballclub or a rebuilding one. It's a long process. Patience is required. Unfortunately, there is not a lot of patience in pro sports. You have to win games. Period. The thinking of hiring a college coach is that they will bring a new approach and fresh ideas to the pro level.

Hoiberg's Bulls tenure began with a 42-40 record, missing the playoffs by two games. The Bulls did some heavy lifting in the 2016 off-season, signing Dwyane Wade to a two-year deal. The Bulls also brought in veteran point guard Rajon Rondo. The two would join Jimmy Butler, who was on the verge of becoming an elite, top-tier NBA talent.

Just a word on Butler. He was the 30th pick in the 2011 draft. He played in only 42 games his rookie season, averaging 8 minutes a game. He watched and took everything in, and then played in all 82 games the following season. Jimmy won the trust of Coach Thibs, who admired Butler's work ethic especially on the defensive side of the ball.

My interaction with NBA players is brief. I have a job to do and they're respectful, granting me interviews. I am not personal friends with players; they're young enough to be my sons! But I saw something in Butler that made me approach him early in his second season—something I have done only once. Prior to a game at the United Center I said, "Jimmy, you have raw talent, and if you put it together and want this bad enough, you're going to have a terrific career. I love your heart, drive, grit, toughness, and fearlessness." He thanked me for the encouragement and that was it. It was a fifteen-second exchange.

His All-Star status is not a reflection of anything I said, but I wanted to encourage him and challenge him. He didn't need anyone or anything to motivate him, certainly not from a play-by-play announcer, but I liked his passion very much. I like being around people who aren't afraid to fail by taking risks. Butler wanted it badly. He blossomed into an All Star, but that also meant Hoiberg had to deal with three "Alphas" in Butler, Rondo, and Wade. The three players wanted the ball in their hands at crunch time and embraced pressure.

January 25, 2017. The Bulls led Atlanta 110-100 with 3:02 remaining only to see the Hawks outscore the Bulls 19-4 to end the game. Atlanta won 119-114. Fans were upset; everyone was upset. I was in the Bulls locker room after the game waiting to interview Butler and Wade for Bulls TV. Both players are great interviews, but there was something about the loss that turned the locker room into complete silence. We waited and waited and waited.

Both frustrated veterans finally addressed the media and offered their views on the meltdown.

Dwayne Wade said: "I can look at Jimmy and say Jimmy's doing his job. Jimmy can look at me and say Dwayne's doing his job. I don't know if we can keep going down the line and be able to say that." (The Athletic)

Wade also offered more opinions directed at some of the young players on the Bulls roster: "Losses like this, it has to hurt them. I'm 35 years old, man. I got three championships. It shouldn't hurt me more than it hurts these young guys. They have to want it." (The Athletic)

With Butler and Wade offering their opinions in a transparent, raw kind of manner, Rajon Rondo, who won a ring with the Celtics in 2008, penned a social media response on Instagram pertaining to postgame remarks from Butler and Wade. He said: "My vets (referring to Paul Pierce and Kevin Garnett) would never go to the media. When we lost, they wouldn't blame us. They took responsibility and got in the gym. They showed the young guys what it meant to work."

Rondo said it was unfair to blame the team's less experienced players. "The young guys work," he wrote. "They show up. They don't deserve blame. If anything is questionable, it's the leadership."

Bulls management fined all three players an undisclosed amount of money.

It was not a good look. Some things are best left unsaid. This was such a case.

The irony of the 2016-17 season is the Bulls finished the year at 41-41 and claimed the eighth seed in the Eastern Conference via a tiebreaker with Miami. The Bulls would face the top seed Boston Celtics in the opening round. The Bulls won the first two games of the series on the road and appeared to be in a strong position to upset the Celtics and advance.

Out of nowhere, on the team's off day prior to game three, it was revealed that Rondo had suffered a fractured right thumb in the second half of game two and would be sidelined for weeks. Without Rondo the Celtics stormed back, winning four straight and capturing the series in six games. Had Rondo been healthy there is no doubt in my mind the Bulls would have overtaken the mighty Celtics.

The Bulls elected to change things up in the off-season. Wade agreed to a buyout, making his stay in Chicago a brief one. I'll say this for Wade, he was total class and got heavily involved off the court with a number of worthwhile charitable causes. Rondo was waived, making his stay a brief one as well. Rondo has a terrific feel for the game.

Butler was dealt on draft night to Minnesota in a blockbuster deal that sent Kris Dunn, Zach LaVine, and the draft rights to Lauri Markkanen to the Bulls. The Butler era in Chicago was over.

It's easy to second guess the Bulls five years later, but a change of scenery had to happen for both parties. Everyone respects Butler's work ethic. He's a terrific guy and his outstanding career is now in conversation for the Hall of Fame.

Meantime, LaVine has blossomed into an All Star under Billy Donovan and earned himself the largest contract ever given to a player in Bulls history. LaVine still hasn't reached his ceiling. He is so gifted and fluid as a player.

Billy Donovan was the right coach at the right time for LaVine. Billy has taken the Thunder and Bulls to the playoffs in six of his seven years in the NBA. Donovan is an outstanding teacher. It's vital that a coach can teach and communicate.

As the 2010 free agency period hit July 1, Bulls VP John Paxson asked me if I'd assist in their efforts to recruit Chris Bosh to Chicago. Bosh had played out his contract with the Raptors and was ready to test the market. During my time in Toronto I had a terrific relationship with Chris and would have loved to have seen him in a Bulls uniform playing alongside Rose, Noah, and Deng. Chris is intelligent, articulate, thoughtful, and a man of great character.

I landed in his hometown of Dallas ready to meet Chris and his family. With the embargo lifted at 12:01 a.m., I was the first to arrive in a torrential rainstorm as I navigated my way through a posh gated community. Slowly, one by one, long stretch limousines pulled up. I knocked on the door and presented Chris with an iPad as every team did back then, with several apps showcasing the team, city, and his marketability should he sign with the Bulls. I also tossed in for good measure my daughter's chocolate chip cookies, which he had enjoyed since he arrived in the NBA in 2003.

We had a brief chat while the entire presentation was being filmed by someone in his palatial home. Chris trusted me, and there was no way I would do anything to damage our friendship. Relationships above all else. I wanted him to wear a Bulls uniform. Period. But we know how history played out as he formed the "Big 3" in Miami with Wade and LeBron James, winning multiple titles. He was elected to the Hall of Fame in 2021 following a brilliant career. In my heart I truly believe had Bosh signed with the Bulls he would have been a more featured player than he was in Miami, and the Bulls would have won a title or two with him, Rose, Noah, and Deng.

I called John Paxson's last college basketball game. Ironically, it was St. Patrick's Day, March 17, 1983, as his Irish lost to Northwestern in an NIT tournament game at the then-named Rosemont Horizon. But my relationship with John really began with his arrival in Chicago in 1985. I loved his game at Notre Dame, and it was a perfect fit when GM Jerry Krause brought him to the Bulls. Pax was an old-school player who was tough, smart, and a consummate team player. He would do anything for the team and never had an agenda. I saw Paxson take on quicker, more athletic point guards and not back down to any of them.

NBA history will tell you the biggest shot of his career came in game six of the 1993 Finals against the Suns when he buried a left wing three ball with 3.9 seconds left as the Bulls captured their third straight title 99-98. All this is true. But don't forget the fourth quarter of game five in the '91 Finals. With the Lakers smothering Michael Jordan, Head Coach Phil Jackson told MJ, "You've got an open man, pass it to Paxson." Paxson delivered.

Like all executives, Paxson had some hits and some misses

in the Bulls front office, but overall I thought he did a solid job. I think Paxson was ready to turn the page when he elected to step down as VP of Basketball Operations. This is a nonstop 365, 24-7 job. It takes a toll on your mind, heart, and spirit. It's all-consuming. No one cares more about the Bulls than Paxson. Of course, I'm very biased about Pax. He's one of the best guys I've ever met, and his heart is in the right place.

Paxson built a Bulls team around Derrick Rose. It appeared to be working as the Bulls readied themselves for the opening game of the first round of the 2012 playoffs against the Philadelphia 76ers (coached by former Bulls Head Coach Doug Collins). In a truncated schedule due to a lockout, the Bulls stormed through the Eastern Conference going 50-16. Rose played in only 39 games that season, dealing with an assortment of injuries ranging from toe, back, groin, and feet issues. The Bulls jumped on the 76ers, and with 1:12 remaining in the fourth quarter with the Bulls leading by 12 points, Rose crumpled to the floor in front of the 76ers bench after making a non-contact play.

Rose was in agony clutching his left knee. You could have heard a pin drop as 21,943 at the United Center held their collective breath hoping it was a minor injury. It wasn't. He was assisted off the floor by the Bulls medical staff. During a commercial break, Bill Wennington told me it's not going to be good. After the game there was still no official word on Rose's injury. I was glued to the radio on the way back home, but no word yet on Rose's status.

I went to 5 p.m. Mass at St. Michael's Church in Wheaton. I turned down the volume on my phone, but 20 minutes into the service there was a murmur swirling around church. I reached for my phone and saw the news: Derrick Rose had suffered a torn ACL in his left knee. Short term/long term it wasn't good news, and quite honestly the Bulls never recovered from Rose's injury.

Rose missed a full season only to have another setback, this to his right knee, suffering a torn MCL against Portland on November 22, 2013. But when I think of Rose's career in Chicago it's only good things. Rookie of the Year. All Star. Youngest player in NBA history at 22 to win the MVP. No Bulls' player has worn Rose's jersey number 1 since he was dealt to the Knicks in 2016.

I like Derrick very much. He is always polite, respectful, and kind to me. I can't say one negative word about him. His run with the Bulls provided some of the most enjoyable seasons I've spent as a broadcaster. Unfortunately, Rose's injury, coupled with Miami's dominance, meant the Bulls just couldn't make inroads in the Eastern Conference.

It was time to turn the page.

The 2022-23 season will be my 25th calling NBA games.

Here is what I've learned watching NBA basketball all these years. A team must be healthy come mid-April. Character is everything. Players must know their roles. The 11th man on the roster can't complain about playing time. It can be disruptive to the chemistry of the locker room. Your top offensive players should be engaged defensively. Your top players should be willing to be coached and willing to take constructive criticism. It's a grind. By the time the playoffs start it's a given that your top eight players are dealing with some kind of physical pain. But there's a difference between being hurt and being injured. If you're hurt, you play. Teams have to play through it. Simple as that. And players have to maintain their love of the game.

I am a huge proponent of having kids play multiple sports. It develops other muscles, and a change gives them a different outlook on sports to begin with. The last thing you want is to take away the joy of the game by burning out a kid who's in the gym 24-7. The human body can only take so much pressure on different levels.

As for the Bulls? They are back on track developing a culture that will sustain them for seasons to come. The Bulls have an excellent coach in Billy Donovan and a fantastic set of assistants. Arturas Karnisovas, Marc Eversley, and the entire front office staff will remain aggressive, bringing Chicago a consistent winning team. Their goal will remain focused on capturing an NBA championship.

CHAPTER 13
COMING IN FROM THE BULLPEN

In May of 2015 I received a call from White Sox Vice President Brooks Boyer inquiring whether I would be willing to sit in for Sox legend Hawk Harrelson while Harrelson was away for two weeks. My first thought was not to accept the flattering offer. I had not called a baseball game since 1979. Boyer assured me that the organization had complete confidence in my work, so it was full speed ahead.

I was definitely outside of my comfort zone.

What got me through the 17-game stretch was the support and work turned in by Sox analyst Steve Stone. I had known Steve for years, but this was a different venue altogether. Steve is the absolute best at what he does and how he does it. He is as good as it gets. My game plan was to feature Steve as much as possible and make him the star in the booth. I asked plenty of questions and knew my role, my strengths, and my weaknesses.

As I often tell young broadcasters, "Just be you. No one else. Be you." I needed to listen to my own voice, which I did. I had to not only learn the history and tendencies of Sox players but also the opposition. The Sox staff was outstanding, as were the players. GM Rick Hahn is a first-class individual. I met some new people along the way, ranging from A.J. Hinch, then of the Astros, who was extremely patient, informative, and kind to me, to John Gibbons, then manager of the Blue Jays, who gave me great stories prior to the Blue Jays series. Former Orioles catcher turned TV analyst Rick Dempsey, who caught Stone back in the day, also gave me plenty of fantastic intel on the nuances of calling a game and framing pitches. I had to know the rule book and the dimensions of ballparks. My new best friend was MLB TV.

Sox Director of Broadcasting Bob Grim was extremely gracious with his time, providing constructive criticism and being there for me 24-7. In 2016 and 2017 I did a game or two as my run ended with the emergence of a bright young superstar in the making, Jason Benetti. My work was well received by the Sox and Sox fans and that's all I needed.

I like to stay busy, and I like to work. I am truly blessed. In my combined 30 years in Chicago I have called play-by-play and public address for the Chicago Bulls, play-by-play for the Chicago White Sox, play-by-play and public address for the Chicago Sting, anchored pre- and post-shows on the Cubs radio network and public address for the Cubs, broadcast DePaul basketball play-by-play, and called TV football and basketball for Northwestern and hosted the Francis Peay Show (football). I've also anchored pre-intermission and post for the Chicago Blackhawks (1979-80), hosted sports talk shows on WCFL (first Chicago weeknight sports talk show), WLUP, WGN, and several on 670 The Score, hosted pre-half-post shows on Bears radio network, and even one game of public address for the Chicago Bears.

I have been honored, humbled, and grateful with three inductions into Halls of Fame: The Chicagoland Sports Hall of Fame, the Illinois Basketball Coaches Association Hall of Fame, and the WGN Radio Walk of Fame. The truth is awards and accolades come and go. Hardware tarnishes with time, games come and go, but the heart and soul of humankind leaves a legacy forever.

My goal every day is to be a better man in every way possible.

MENTORS

Mentoring is extremely important regardless of your career path. It's paramount to gravitate to people of character, integrity, and selflessness. Five individuals come to mind who shaped my standard of professional values: Roger Ringstad, Joe Tait, Vince Bagli, Pete Gross, and Ernie Harwell.

Earlier in the book I mentioned the impact Gross and Tait had on my life. Now a little about Roger Ringstad, Vince Bagli, and Ernie Harwell.

Roger Ringstad held a dual role at Interlake High School serving as the school's Vice Principal and Athletic Director. He was a very good man and one with great morals and ethics. Prior to my ninth-grade academic year at IHS, on the suggestion of my mom, I showed up unannounced at the school one July morning. I was surprised to find him in the office midsummer but then again, the man was dedicated. I told him I'd like to voluntarily assist the athletic department any way I could.

He looked at me like I was a zombie! Here's a 14-year-old kid who hasn't taken one high school class showing up in the Vice Principal's office eagerly hoping to do anything sports-related. To his credit, Ringstad took me to a large room with at least fifty football helmets. He pointed to a box of soft cloths and cleaning spray and said have at it. I took pride in each helmet. I wanted those helmets to shine. I've always been task-oriented, a trait from my parents, and if the job at hand was to clean and polish helmets, so be it. But it had to be done correctly. Once that assignment was over it was time to hang football jerseys and practice pants. I did this until school started in early September. I would show up twice weekly and there was always something to do. I appreciate what Roger Ringstad did for me. I drove him crazy, no doubt, but he knew my heart was in the right place. He was a straight arrow. When I look back on my high school years. Roger Ringstad immediately comes to mind.

In 1967, a year after my father died, my uncle who lived in Baltimore introduced me to Vince Bagli, an iconic sportscaster in the area. Not once in my 50-year friendship with Mr. Bagli did I ever refer to him as Vince. I totally respected and revered the man. His passing in 2021 is felt to this day. Vince was an incredible human being. He showed interest in everyone, and he remembered their names. He'd see a driver who delivers milk and would say, "Hey George, how are you?" He had an unbelievable recall of dates and events and knew Baltimore better than anyone.

The Bagli family invited me into their home for a number of years. I would accompany Mr. Bagli to and from the station. I'd find things to do and never left his side. It was an incredible experience. I'd attend Orioles games, Colts training camp, and other events.

In late June 1967, Mr. Bagli surprised me with a huge thrill. My mom had taught White Sox pitcher Bruce Howard in high school in Virginia. He was a promising pitcher in the Sox system and by all accounts was a future top-tier rotation pitcher for the White Sox. When my mom told me about Howard, I began to follow his career from his days in the minor leagues. On this particular day, Mr. Bagli and I went to a Baltimore hotel to grab an "interview."

I was shocked when Howard walked through the lobby and introduced himself to me. My jaw dropped and my knees were shaking. I was meeting my first ever major league player—not just a major league player but someone who had a connection to my family. The three of us had breakfast and I can still remember what Howard ordered: scrambled eggs, bacon, and toast. Howard was traded the following season to the Orioles in a major trade involving Luis Aparicio, who was heading back to the White Sox. Unfortunately, Howard suffered an arm injury with the Orioles and retired soon after.

During the 1968 baseball All Star break, the Bagli family was in the process of moving to a new house. As we were putting stain on a staircase in an empty house, the next-door neighbor frantically rushed into the house and said, "Vince, you have a phone call." He left and returned moments later, telling me our day was over. The Orioles had fired manager Hank Bauer, replacing him with coach Earl Weaver. The next day I stood next to the new manager of the Baltimore Orioles, Earl Weaver, as he was being interviewed by Vince Bagli in a Baltimore hotel. The rest is history. Honest to God, true story. Weaver became one of the game's greatest managers and is in the Hall of Fame.

Bagli had an outstanding relationship with Baltimore athletes. One July morning in 1967 I was reading the sports section of the Baltimore Sun at the Bagli residence when I heard a knock on the door. Who walks right in? None other than Brooks Robinson. Robinson was a superstar and here he was a foot away from me telling me they're running late for a tee time.

I stayed in touch with Mr. Bagli throughout the years. I saw him for the final time in 2015 when I called a White Sox-Orioles game in Baltimore. He came up to the booth, put the headset on, and heard me broadcast a major league game. It was one of the best moments of my life.

I met members of the Baltimore Colts at training camp like Johnny Unitas, Tom Matte, Lenny Moore, Art Donovan, and other Colts greats. When the Jets upset the Colts in Super Bowl III, I cried. Kevin Loughery of the then Baltimore Bullets was a friend of Bagli, and wouldn't you know it, Loughery later became head coach of the Bulls for two seasons and was Michael Jordan's first NBA coach. Loughery would leave me tickets when he would come to Seattle as an active player. George Young who worked for the Colts and later became a Hall of Fame General Manager of the New York Giants was a dear friend of the Bagli family and was a frequent guest at their home. I overheard Young tell him the Colts were ready to make a major trade that would send Bubba Smith to the Raiders for Raymond Chester. Sure enough, it happened.

When I reflect on my relationship with Vince Bagli, I see God's hands all over it. For someone such as myself, who lost his father a year before meeting him, knowing how much sports and sports broadcasting meant to me, to be staying in his house, going to work with him, attending games, and meeting people that would become lifelong friends, it's pretty clear. You may think it's a lucky break. I don't. I think, check that, I know God put His hands on me that very moment. Vince Bagli was a great, great man.

Another incredible mentor in my life was Ernie Harwell. Vince Bagli introduced me to the Tigers broadcaster in 1967. Prior to arriving in Detroit in 1960, Harwell had previously called Orioles games. Ernie, much like Vince, was a gentleman full of humility and kindness. I saw Ernie every summer during my trips to Baltimore when the Tigers came to play. We would speak by phone once a month and he always had time for me. Always.

The Tigers championship season of 1968 was a memorable one for Ernie as he called a World Series winner, just as he later did in 1984. But Harwell's Hall of Fame career spanned decades of greatness. I was in attendance on July 27, 1968, in Baltimore when Tigers Cy Young Award winner Denny McClain won his 20th of his Major League-leading 31 games in a 9-0 shutout. Think about that. McClain won his 20th game in late July. He started 41 games that season, completing 28. That's right, 28 complete games. Today, if a starting pitcher can give you six innings, he can make a boatload of money. Baseball has certainly changed.

I was with Ernie the entire day when he broadcast his last game. It took place September 29, 2002, in Toronto. Again, God's hands were all over this. I was living and working in Toronto and of all the cities to finish Harwell's brilliant career…Toronto. The Tigers lost 1-0 to the Blue Jays, but the game on the field was insignificant. It was all about Ernie. I was in the booth the entire game. We walked out of the SkyDome together and I really didn't know what to say. Here's a man that called Major League Baseball for over 50 years, and it was over. What a life. The Brooklyn Dodgers thought so highly of Harwell they traded catcher Cliff Dapper to the minor league Atlanta Crackers of the Southern Association for Harwell's broadcasting contract. My favorite Harwell phrase was following a called third strike: "He stood there like the house by the side of the road." Classic!

Ernie was beloved by everyone, and our world was a better place with his presence. Here was a man I met in 1967 as a 13-year-old, reaching out and encouraging me to take a sports position at WJR Radio 27 years later. How crazy is that? Our friendship grew even closer as we spoke nearly daily. I knew Ernie for 43 years and he was a model of consistency throughout every phase of my life.

I saw Ernie about four months before he passed in 2010. He knew the end was near and was at peace, as he was a man of deep faith in Jesus Christ. Ernie and I often talked about our faith, our challenges, our joys, and of course, baseball.

He was one of a kind and always had time for people.

FINAL THOUGHTS

A few closing comments if I may.

I promised myself that one day if given the opportunity, I would create a healthy working environment for both men and women and people of color to take their first step in their journey of pursuing a broadcasting career by receiving internships. I have been blessed to work and to be associated with so many incredibly gifted individuals throughout the years. There are just too many to name.

I never asked an intern to do things I wouldn't do myself. I wanted each and every intern to experience the emotion, pressure, joy, and challenges of the day in-day out life of sports broadcasting. I allowed interns to have the ability to attend games, meet athletes, coaches, and sports personalities, but also be involved and have input in the direction of our sports department. Regardless of the platform, regardless of if they elected to stay in the business or not, each intern that served under my watch received the same amount of respect that I gave high-ranking executives in the broadcast industry. There was no dichotomy whatsoever. Never underestimate the power of internships. For young people, I urge you to network, communicate, and build relationships at an early age in your quest to establish a solid foundation in whatever field you elect to enter.

The radio/television industry is a very small circle of extremely gifted personalities. Case in point. On January 31, 2018, WLS Radio moved on from its radio rights agreement with the Bulls and White Sox.

Normally matters of this nature are handled in the off-season, never in season. In a span of several days the Bulls were able to come to a rights agreement with 670 The Score, Chicago's most listened-to all sports radio station. WSCR's Operations Director Mitch Rosen orchestrated the transition, and it went smoothly.

The was the same Mitch Rosen who had served an internship at WGN Radio in 1988. Mitch's meteoric rise to the top as a radio executive started with an internship. The rest was up to him to pursue his dream and do it in a professional, respectful, and kind way. He is an icon in the sports talk industry and will go down as one of the greatest radio executives, not only in Chicago broadcasting history, but in the United States. Radio needs more people like Mitch Rosen.

Our Bulls radio engineer Rich Wyatt is another example of an employee that always thinks "team" first. His heart, passion, drive, and spirit are contagious. Without question, he is an integral part of our presentation.

More thoughts:

Best sportscaster in Chicago history: Jack Brickhouse

Best baseball player in my lifetime: Willie Mays

Best football player in my lifetime: Tom Brady

Best hockey player in my lifetime: Bobby Orr

Best basketball player in my lifetime: Michael Jordan

Best coach in my lifetime: Scotty Bowman

Best sportscaster in my lifetime: Al Michaels

Best baseball announcers in my lifetime: Jack Buck, Ernie Harwell, Vin Scully

Best football announcers (in alphabetical order): Joe Buck, Ian Eagle, Kevin Harlan, Gus Johnson, Al Michaels, Mike Tirico

Best basketball announcers: (in alphabetical order) Marv Albert, Mike Breen, Jim Durham, Neil Funk, Joe Tait. I also take great pride in seeing women such as Hall of Famer Doris Burke, Lisa Byington (Bucks), Sarah Kustok and Kate Scott (76ers) emerge as top-tier NBA broadcasters. They are pioneers and are exceptional.

Best hockey announcer: Mike Emrick

Best television studio hosts: Bob Costas and Mike Tirico

Best sportswriter in my lifetime: Red Smith

If I could pick one pitcher to win game seven of the World Series: Sandy Koufax

Best single sporting event I ever attended: Super Bowl XX, Bears vs Patriots, January 26, 1986

Greatest game I've ever called: Kobe Bryant, 81 points. Raptors-Lakers. January 22, 2006

Best baseball park: Fenway Park

Best football stadium: Michigan Stadium

Best basketball/hockey arena: United Center

Best sports book: *Strawberries in the Wintertime* by Red Smith

Best sports movie: *Field of Dreams*

Best advice someone gave me: Blues singer Dick Mackey: "You better take care of your homework. If you don't, somebody will."

Pregame broadcast ritual: A prayer of thanksgiving and gratitude along with listening to Elton John's "I'm Still Standing"

Predictions:

Jason Benetti will call multiple World Series games and one day will be inducted into the Baseball Hall of Fame. He will also call a college football national championship game. He will be the primary play-by-play announcer for Fox.

Adam Amin will call multiple World Series/Super Bowl games for Fox.

Young voices to remember: Connor Clark, Bryan Fenley, Jack Kizer, Mike Monaco, Caroline Pineda, Jason Ross Jr., and Chris Vosters.

In closing, I want to thank viewers and listeners over the years for their support, words of encouragement, and kindness. I am not perfect. I have stumbled and fallen many times in my professional and personal life, but I continue to persevere knowing God's mercy and grace blankets me with His love. Thank you to my family, for without them I am nothing.

Always a pleasure!

ABOUT THE AUTHOR

Chuck Swirsky is an award-winning NBA announcer who has spent the last 25 years calling games for the Chicago Bulls and Toronto Raptors.

Swirsky began his professional broadcasting career in 1976 after graduating from Ohio University. He later served as Sports Director at two major radio stations: WGN in Chicago and WJR in Detroit.

In Chicago, Swirsky called basketball play-by-play for DePaul University and the Chicago Sting soccer club, along with hosting pre- and post-game shows on the Chicago Cubs and Chicago Bears radio network. In addition, Swirsky did the television play-by-play for Northwestern University football and handled public address for the Sting, Bulls, and Cubs. He has been inducted into the Chicagoland Sports Hall of Fame, The Illinois Basketball Coaches Hall of Fame, and the WGN Radio Walk of Fame. On September 30, 1994, the Governor of Illinois proclaimed Chuck Swirsky Day for the state.

In Detroit, Swirsky anchored pre, half, and post-game shows on the University of Michigan football network and called the play-by-play for the men's basketball program. He also hosted pre- and post-game shows on the Detroit Tigers and Detroit Red Wings radio network. He was awarded Best Play-by-Play Sportscaster and received Best Sportscast award for the state of Michigan.

Swirsky has also been a guest instructor at the University of Mississippi.

Always a Pleasure is his first book.

OTHER BOOKS FROM ECKHARTZ PRESS

Every Cub Ever

Your Dime My Dance Floor

Chili Dog MVP

Behind the Glass

Ike and Me

Cubsessions

Transatlantic Passage

Signature Shoes

Best Seat in the House